Dedication

Above all else is a deep and abundant gratitude for my children and their partners who altered their lives entirely to ensure that no part of our future generations would encompass an unhealed past. My children tackled their anger, sadness and fears to grow themselves in the process of healing. And we are all the better for the choices made to encourage each other in big and bold ways.

Thank you Goose, Rojo and Slipper for being the kind of humans I'm fortunate to have grown in my body and put on this earth.

CONTENTS

Agents of Social Change

Shifting & Eradicating the Inequities Plaguing Our World Today

Caroline Markel

ISBN: 979-8-218-55208-4

INTRODUCTION

"He threw hot coffee in my face."

I was sitting in the offices of the Jackson County, Missouri, Adult Abuse division. It's an unfortunate office to find yourself in, given the problems and trauma underlying the reasons you ever walk through the door in the first place.

But also, because there is zero privacy. Zero.

So if you go to the office, and seek a restraining order against a person who claimed to love you but only really issued sadness, worry, lies, screaming, fear and pain, you are out in the open. Telling your story, through a speaker in a bullet proof window, to the office people on the other side of the glass.

The entire room can be filled with people, and they now know your full story, too. And your name, because they are going to ask you to spell it, so that they can enter your name into the petition.

I want to be clear on a couple things. For me, this was 2017 and I understand now that you can fill out all the paperwork online for a restraining order. This means the zero-privacy set up has been highly transformed. I also want to note that the people who work in the Jackson County, Missouri, office of Adult Abuse are the most amazing and kind humans I met on my journey navigating the escape from domestic violence. These women answered every question, took my follow-up phone calls, called me back with status reports, and helped me complete forms when I couldn't remember my name.

Seriously. I had to write my name on yellow post-it notes because I couldn't remember my own name. I was wildly traumatized, living in fear, and under duress from his constant texts of, "Don't worry, Sweetpea. I will find you and we will die together." The question, "Tell me your name, please," was met with zero words from my mouth and silent tears.

Which is why on his particular day in 2017, I was becoming increasingly anxious because of the woman sitting next to me.

"He threw hot coffee in my face."

I was back for my second restraining order against the same man I had escaped from in March of 2016. The judge had only given me six months. Insanity! Six months of protection against the most egregious levels of abuse? Insanity.

So here I was again, filling out another round of forms and using my legal insurance benefits through my job at VaxServe Pharmaceuticals, to rehire my lawyer and hope to get another restraining order. I was smarter this time and knew what the routine would be. But it didn't make it any less stressful to sit in that open room and fill out all the paperwork.

"He threw hot coffee in my face. How am I supposed to fill out these forms." She leaned over to me and continued, "I don't even know my own name."

WHOA!!

I was off to the races now with my heart beating so fast. I could smell her fear and sadness because I could constantly smell that foulness as I continued my own fight for personal safety and the safety of my children and pets. The smell is a mixture of sweat after a hard workout from two days prior, and you forgot to change your clothes. Plus, it is mixed with a sweet orange scent. (I was always amazed at the orange scent!) Sometimes, on a really bad day, you could pick up the notes of dog poop smeared on your left shoe. Literal shit reflecting the shit show life had become, aka fear on steroids.

The air suddenly was not breathable, and I could feel my head start to spin. This heightened level of panic always means a screaming train whistle in my ears, and purple blotches breaking out all over my body.

I felt like I was going to pass out, so I grabbed up all my paperwork and purse, and ran out of the room. I didn't even try to answer the woman whose husband of thirty years had thought that it was ok to take an entire pitcher of hot coffee, on a random Tuesday morning, and throw the contents in her face.

I ran. I ran out of the open office. I ran down the hall. I vomited in the bathroom (which was the only way to make the purple blotches on my skin calm the hell down) and I sat on the toilet seat and cried. Ugly tears. Fear-fueled tears. Rage tears.

Afterwards, I planned to leave immediately. So, as soon as I could compose myself, I gathered my things and walked toward the steps to leave.

But I paused at the door of the Adult Abuse office. I walked past it. Paused at the top of the steps. Turned around, opened the door, and walked back in.

She was still there. Zero paperwork completed. Blank stare.

I took back my seat next to her.

And started to cry again.

I told her I was so sorry for what happened to her. I told her that I often couldn't remember my name, either. I told her that this process is hard, but that the ladies are very kind and will help her fill out the paperwork. I then took out the entire contents of my purse, and every contact I had made who helped me in the previous six months. I gave it all to her.

And as I turned around to leave again, I gave her parting words of advice. "When you go to court, dress really nice. Not like you're going to a wedding, but more like you're going to church on Saturday night. Do your hair. Put on a bit of lipstick and a smidge of blush. Look at the judge, not at the man who abused you. Tell the judge how scared you are, and that you are asking for his help to protect you. Thank the judge for listening to you and reading your request."

I could feel myself needing to vomit again, so I left quickly and ran to my car for safety. I'd rather throw up on the side of the road, than spend one more minute in that building. Besides, leaning over the side of the car means zero fear of my long blonde hair hitting the gross toilet seat. Safety in vomiting- never knew this was a lesson I would learn in my life.

I didn't leave my parking space at the courthouse for another 30 minutes; because I couldn't stop crying, and I couldn't catch my breath.

My biggest regret that day? What I didn't do.

I was filled with my own fear and shame. I was livid with myself. I knew what I should have done, and to this day, I can get emotional over what I didn't do.

I should have moved closer to her and sat myself in the open end of the gray, double-wide chair next to her. I should have asked if it was ok for me to take her hand. If she was open to being touched, I should have held her hand and looked her in the eyes. I would have told her that no matter what, never, not ever, is it ok for someone to throw hot coffee in her face or hurt her in any way. I would have reminded her that she is not alone, and there is help.

And it is in this moment that the tagline for Safe In Harm's Way was born:

"Join me. Take my hand, and let's go change the world."

I made a huge promise to myself that I could never leave another person without a hand to hold, if they wanted it. Skin connection with a caring person immediately releases oxytocin and allows the body to be calmed and relaxed. Holding hands can actually reduce inflammation, and lower heart rate and stress. There is so much comfort and progress when a person agrees to hold your hand.

The purpose of this book is to bring all the hand holding to life. Thanks for being here and joining us in the journey. All the chapters written, both as individuals and as corporations, are all related because one person decided to ask people to join her in the journey.

Join me. Take my hand, and let's go change the world.

It's me. It's my attempt to rectify the opportunity I missed in the Adult Abuse office. I wanted a way to positively impact other lives on a massive scale, via an anthology book, and bring to life the real people who connected, and then went on to create change as it relates to domestic violence.

These connections can be an example to any reader or their ability to show up authentically and create change; especially when the world seems heavy and complicated. The question becomes a version of, "I'm only one person. What can one person do?"

The reality is one person can create ripples of change when they authentically connect person by person; and then those people connect with others and create change, too. Life becomes an ever-expanding web of goodness.

This book is filled with the authentic connections that were made as I built two world-wide companies to address the $3.6 trillion dollar problem of domestic violence. And what I love about each author is that there is really no reason I should even know them or be working with them. Except I am. Except I do.

Because I made a choice to heal out loud and lessen my own silence and shame by sharing my story of escaping domestic violence, under the daily cloud of text messages promising me, "Don't worry, Sweetpea. I will find you and we will die together." And I learned that sharing my story helped other people share their story, plus gave them the courage to seek safety and healing.

But what I didn't count on was the beautiful momentum that healing brought me in connecting with others. New people in my life who believed in my mission as much as I did, and offered their friendship, time, and talent to make my own dreams come true.

I count these people, our shared story, and their own personal stories as miracles. Because while there is no reason, I should be working with them and know them so well (except for the fact that I chose to escape violence.) There is no reason they should know each other. Except now they do.

As we continue to create an ever-expanding web of goodness, I hope these stories inspire you where you need it most. I hope you decide to start connecting as your true self and know down to your soul that the right people will come along. Promise. The minute you let go of the people and beliefs which no longer serve you, the faster the right people will come along.

Take Hayley Lewis, I met Hayley randomly, courtesy of the Dave Matthews Band. Dave Matthews and Tim Reynolds were playing in Cancun, Mexico for three nights on the beach in January of 2017. Despite worrying about traveling by myself, I committed to making new friends and met Hayley in the process. We both joined a Facebook group for the trip and made the connection of living just a couple miles from each other in Kansas City.

Let me tell you a bit about Hayley. She shows up. Even when she is nervous and would rather be home with her pets, she shows up and walks through any door for the people she loves. All 98 pounds of her comes in and wraps her arms around you, no matter what her own day is bringing. If I am having a garage sale to earn cash for Safe In Harm's Way, she is there at 5:00 am to help set up and stays to clean up at 5:30 pm. Every birthday party and baby shower- there. I need help with accounting issues, she will copy and categorize every transaction. The courage this woman brings to the world astounds me. She isn't perfect, and she is often quick to point out her own faults; but I wouldn't trade her friendship for any other version of all the glory in her.

It brings me wild joy to talk about our next author, Kim Ring. I have known Kim her entire life. Kim attended the same school as my children and was their after-school babysitter. I kept tabs on Kim as life evolved, but there were many years in between of disconnection. Until I started to follow her on Facebook and learned she had become a powerhouse in the public relations world within the cannabis industry. This highly intelligent and beautiful creature was building her own brand and organization, and making amazing things happen as a female-founded entrepreneur in a new industry emerging across the United States.

Let me give you a sneak peak of Kim. You really need to understand her super cool-chick vibe and energy, because it is a whirlwind which attracts other people to all endeavors. Need to get an invite to a red-carpet event? No fear, Kim walks in and acts like she owns the place, and people would not dare think otherwise. She is inquisitive and asks great questions, plus doesn't flinch when feedback needs to be given. Kim is the reason Safe In Harm's Way has been featured in multiple top-tier publications like Forbes and Ms. Magazine. She is the reason we have secured premier airtime with television news stations. Kim takes our data and outcomes, creates incredible copy, and networks with only the best people to ensure our services for survivors of domestic violence get attention. Pro Bono for five years- never charging us one penny for her dedication and effort, because she believes in the mission so fiercely.

You're also going to get to know Sheri Kurdakul. There are so many warm and fuzzy feelings to have about Sheri. I tell her all the time, before meeting her and talking to her for about 90 minutes at our very first real introduction, I just thought she was the coolest kid on the playground. And really wondered how I could get her to be my friend. It has everything to do with the way her brain works to come up with things and thinks outside the box.

She is going to be talking about her journey of creating VictimsVoice, and I'd never want to steal that part of the story. Let's just suffice it to say that Sheri developed the only cloud-based system in the United States which allows survivors of violence to document their abuse in formats allowing people to have their experience admissible in court. She truly saves lives, and if all my wishes are to be granted, the biggest wish is to keep being her friend. I just want to keep doing the things that mean the most with her. I want to keep jumping rope with her during recess, on the playground of advocacy work. (And when I once told this to her, she responded, "I don't really like to jump rope, but we could figure out something else to play on the playground. That'd be great.") So that's just my goal is to keep being able to hang out with Sheri in any way. I'm sure once you meet her in this book, you'll want to join in on our recess dates, too.

I think you're also going to love Tracy Rector. I feel like Tracy's always been in my life. As I was preparing to write about Tracy, I was thinking, what was our origin? Was it LinkedIn? Was it a conference? I can't recall which is the best kind of memory for me, because it makes me feel like I've always been lucky to have her around. There is some chemistry to us which aligns despite our different pathways, and geographies.

We share our stories differently in healing out loud, plus our stories are completely different! Completely different, yet inter-woven connections and "Oh!!!! Me, too!" moments. But I think we both have this energy that we bring to the table- an energy and passion which makes other people want to be around us. There is nothing which makes me prouder, then watching Tracy share her story to a room full of hundreds of people, and each person responds to her. Turn around, and she will be surrounded by folks who just want to talk to her more. It's a beautiful thing. I'm just so in awe of all the connections she makes, and all the awareness she is raising; it's really incredible.

If you can imagine a spotlight set to super shine, it would need to be directed to Jenn Toro. I met Jenn the first time I ever decided to creep back out into the world. It was at an event called Linkedin Live. I had gotten all dressed up to go, and my son thought I was headed to a date. Nope- I was petrified to be in public, and the only armor which gave me courage was a cute dress, lipstick and heels.

Jenn helped organize the event, and she stood on the stage to give this amazing speech. I remember coming home thinking I'm going to be courageous, and I'm going to send her a message that says how impressed I was by her. Flash forward to 2023, and she is my plus-one on most of the big events in Kansas City. In fact, I recently received an invite to a huge gala, and the woman who invited me said, "Please bring whoever you want, but I'm hoping it's Jenn Toro, because you ladies have so much fun together."

And we do! But we also have really deep conversations lasting hours, or sometimes just a three-minute voice message. Jenn's energy is this divine light that just makes me think and makes me look at the world differently. I already think I do a really good job of that, but then I talk with Jenn, and she ups the ante on how she authentically invests in people and in the culture, she helps create. I know we have circled each other in different lives and centuries. My hope is that no matter what, she keeps showing up in every version of the lives I live.

My favorite social media platform is LinkedIn. I love the exchanges with people across the globe, and following people who make good sense, create impact, and are not afraid to call things out in need of change. Sybil Cummin is one connection I made on LinkedIn. We bonded over the immense need of resources regarding the court system as a source of secondary abuse for people trying to navigate a "high conflict" divorce, which is just another phrase for domestic violence. If you want to dive deep into changing lives, Sybil does that with her therapy practice. Her focus on children and ensuring their health and safety is second-to-none.

Here is what I see in Sybil. I love that, like myself, when you get her talking about something passionate there could be a curse word or two slip from her mouth. I dig a chick who can curse appropriately. Next, she is a committed friend. Sybil sends me random texts encouraging me to check out new people she has found, and also keeps me posted if she finds research or information, she thinks is impactful. We are all busy, yet Sybil goes out of her way to ensure everyone has access to the latest and greatest information. Finally, she is smart and funny in the most wicked ways of extreme intelligence and comments that make me belly laugh. I will get a text that says, "Hey, can you chat for five minutes, and three hours later, her kids will be running amok because we are still on the phone solving world problems, and giggling like seventh grade girls talking about slumber parties. You're going to love Sybil, and I can't wait for you to read what she has to say!

Dr. Tony Meiners is devoting his chapter to some pretty heavy things faced while growing up. Let me just tell you this, after reading his chapter I wanted to track down every person who has harmed him and inflict some sort of retribution. Honestly. (I'm shaking my head and tearing up as I type this.) I need not worry, though, because karma will take care of anything needed. And karma for Tony? Sobriety. A doctorate degree, crafting a life built on his experiences, but turned into helping people.

And please, follow him on Instagram, because I intend to randomly show up unannounced for one of his spin classes. You'll want to come, too. Better start working out now, and we can be ready by 2025.

I have known Tony since he was born, and while time separated us, it was easy to reconnect because I stated my intentions clearly when I finally worked up the courage to reach out to him again. I asked him to keep studying, keep working hard, and then when he graduated to come and work with me at Safe In Harm's Way. He agreed, and now our conversations and texts end with, "I love you" and all is right in the world because Dr. Meiners is going to make sure we absolutely provide top-notch services for historically marginalized people.

Wrapping up our individual chapters is Amy Impara-Gregory. Amy is the best thing that happened to me from a relationship I left behind. She is the only thing I carried over from that life, and I am a better person for it. Here is the deal about Amy that I love. Amy is always on a pathway of acceptance and true love. She is never afraid to learn new things about herself, and then implement what currently fits her growth and soul. She is inclusive in that she welcomes others on that journey, too.

Amy honors herself so much that she doesn't allow others, who are not on the same pathway of growth that she travels, to compromise her integrity or pathway. Of course, there are moments of questioning; but she always settles into, "What am I meant to learn here?"

I've traveled across the world with this woman, and experienced so many people, places, food and fun. These travels have expanded my own friendship circles because that is also the kind of person she is- inclusive and kind with a focus on expanding everyone's ability, friendships, and experiences. Additionally, she is an incredible dancer and singer, which brings me such great joy. Her demeanor comes alive into a vibrant energy when she throws out a song or two and gets down to any ABBA song.

Amy's recent journey has taken a swift turn and alteration to every component of her life in the previous ten years. You're going to love your ring-side seat to her journey.

We have the additional bonus content of highlighting three female-founded entities providing positive impact and change in their respective industries. These Chapters will be a different focus as highlighting corporate entities. I want to provide the intimate vision of the women behind the corporation.

I'm beginning with Courtney Beth Anderson. I met Courtney through my friend Joe. Joe is one of the most stellar humans I have ever met, and I met him when I met Hayley at the Dave Matthews and Tim Reynolds 2017 concert weekend in Mexico. Joe and I have traveled together multiple times to see Dave in concert, and I have had the pleasure of getting to know his family, too. Bonus- in 2018 Joe brought along this lovely addition named Courtney.

I remember first meeting Courtney on the beach, and thinking, "She is so Joe worthy- what a cool chick!" And then the next day we were all meeting together before the concert. We're in this room, and all of a sudden, it's like, "Oh, it's YOU! WOW! You are an intelligent and purpose-driven soul. I need to be friends with YOU!"

It became a moment of "Joe who? Okay, go ahead and leave now Joe. Courtney and I are talking, and because of her focus on health, you can leave now."

I am in awe of this woman intent on healing through food. Plus, she is my partner in music and trust. Trust that timing is right, and there are no limits or expectations except to show up when we can, and how we can, to create opportunities for friendship, love and collaboration. Regardless of how long it is between conversations, I am wildly thankful to be on this journey with Courtney. Courtney's determination to lead with health as a way to heal, will change the world.

Next up is Looped Solutions and the fabulous team that Kara Wasser and her team including Lisa DiMuccio-Zgela have created. They get it. They get the power of connection. Kara has created the focus of, "We understand the importance of having the right contacts and making connections with those who can influence change. We value the relationships we have built today, but also realize it takes a village to make real change. It takes one phone call, one email to the right person that can make all the difference."

The work that is done within Looped Solutions Purple means that people who are navigating the complexities of domestic violence have a secure and safe place to interact with advocates. This means that in the intimate and quiet moments of a survivor's needs, advocates can actively assist with life, family, and safety concerns. It's the difference between shame and silence and life-saving help.

It is a pleasure that my organization, Safe In Harm's Way, works within their app to provide additional resources needed for health, safety, and healing. Personally, Kara has taken the initiative to start a Cool Kids Tech Club- and the kicker is that we are the most inclusive club you'd ever want to join. The ultimate goal? Increase the use of technology to eradicate the normalization of violence. Seriously. The first domestic violence shelter opened around 1972, and I firmly believe MANY advocates are still using systems from that same year. We are going to engage everyone to jet-set up to the current year. NOW.

Our final corporate chapter is written by Jessica McCallop-McClellan. Let me begin with complete transparency, I love the love Jessica and her husband, Kevin, share. They have been at this marriage gig for several decades now, and they are my couple goals. The love and support I witness between the two of them is stellar and something to remind myself about an "after" filled with encouragement, intelligence, and kindness. See them dance? My goodness- it's pure joy to witness.

Now a good love is hard to find, but an incredible female entrepreneur is the kind of achievement which generations can envy and establishes family success. Jessica accomplishes that, too. You will absolutely be compelled to join her mission to end period poverty. Period!

Most important to me personally is Jessica's support and friendship. She refers to me as the blackest white girl she knows- in front of family and friends, or in front of a 45-person non-profit leadership call between two states. Our friendship crosses so many lines, which other people struggle to navigate. Jessica makes it easy because she firmly believes in unity. She also makes it easy because she will randomly call me to pray over me or about my family. Jessica includes me in every big adventure she creates, and I end up being on TV or giving interviews because she wants to ensure every person can shine. When you read about her activities, you will fall in love with the multi-pronged missions to end multiple different needs around the world.

Finally, I need to make one last introduction to Melissa Mansfield-Anderson. I met Melissa in 2020 when we both attended a weekend long event based on learning about digital marketing. I just loved her vibe and the way she authentically interacted with people. Her energy was contagious, and she committed to solidly building fierce female friendships and collaborations. Melissa has been present for every single one of our triumphs at Safe In Harm's Way. She is the emcee premier when we do "live" and active campaigns. She helped us run our social media presence, and even served on our board. There are so many memories which include Melissa, and she is always going to be part of our stellar history.

Melissa is going to be talking about food scarcity in the realms of how violence can extend its ugly hands into the bellies of kids affected by domestic abuse. She is intent on rectifying food scarcity at every level so that kids can grow up safe and fed consistently and without fear of going hungry.

Thanks for being here on the journey. Thank YOU for taking my hand to change the world. If your life currently involves scrolling through Instagram, reading all about the nastiness in the world- know this from the tips of your toes to the top of your head; YOU CAN MAKE A DIFFERENCE ONE PERSON AT A TIME.

Miss your childhood best friend? Send them a message and ask to meet for coffee. Pick out specific things you remember about people and tell them. Don't let your own fear pause yourself and send you running (literally or metaphorically) away in fear and sadness. Maybe you strive to engage in a community close to your own experiences and heart; sign up for their newsletter and actively engage. Start showing up places and say, "Hello." to any person you walk past. Take 1.5 seconds of confidence, and before you know it someone will respond, "Hey. How are you?" BOOM! Off to the moment which could change both your lives.

And if you make a mistake, summon up the courage to walk back into any room you ran from, and start over. Please. It could be the difference between life and death. Karma and retribution. Shame and silence, or courage and conviction.

My hot coffee lady? She ended up being in the courtroom right after my restraining order was granted. I was packing up my purse, and when I turned around, there she was! I stayed and watched her dressed up, but not too dressy, and looking only at the judge, not her sneering hot coffee-throwing husband. She told the judge thank you for reading her filing, and that she was very scared of the man standing across from her, and she asked the judge for help and protection.

She got it!! She got the restraining order!!

As I started to cry, my lawyer asked if I was OK. I told him, "Yes. I am just so very happy for her." He said, "Let's walk to your car together. I want to make sure your ex is not waiting for you and hiding. It's time to get you on the road." And with that, Jim took my hand, and I was instantly calm and less stressed. He walked with me, in yet another moment of courage and connection. Jim waited for my car to start, and me to drive away, before he turned and left in his own car.

One simple action. One world changed.

Join me. Take my hand and let's go change the world.

EMPOWERING MOVE MOMENTS: BRINGING WILDEST DREAMS INTO REALITY

Every single day offers the opportunity to redefine our path and take a significant step toward realizing our wildest dreams. For the past eight years, I've been immersed in the creation of frameworks, systems, and courses that empower individuals to seize these moments—those pivotal "Move Moments" that can shift not only the trajectory of a business but also a life. This chapter is a reflection on those years of work, growth, and dedication, driven by a vision to help people protect their energy, focus their goals, and bring their dreams to fruition.

Three years ago, I embarked on a journey in the digital marketing space, where my mission was clear: to create an atlas for success and safety in the ever-evolving landscape of online business. I understood from the start that achieving dreams required not only ambition but also a clear path forward, shielded from the risks that come with entrepreneurship in a digital world.

This was the direct result of my own corporate journey. I spent twenty-five years in the pharmaceutical sales industry. I achieved excellent results and growth resulting in leading the largest revenue producing unit in an international company. Until one random call at 2 pm cst in October of 2021 found me opening an email from the National Sales Vice President inviting me to a Team's Meeting. This person calls himself as "accomplished, energized, and visionary leader with diverse strengths driving sales force excellence," and with a snap of his fingers I was let go from my position with just four months of severance.

It didn't matter that I had achieved international, company-wide awards and acclaim. It didn't matter that I had conducted field sales training on fostering customer relationships to exceed desired results. My ability to lead webinars with attendees that numbered in the hundreds across the country mattered nothing, nor did my invitations to train employees across the globe on new product offerings.

None of that mattered, and I was instantly dismissed.

Suddenly, all those nights on the road away from family, and the intense commitment to excellence which I displayed (and consequently, earned him bonus money) left me without a paycheck and health insurance. I vowed then that my genesis of bringing my sales skills to a digital platform would be the way to design my own destiny and generational wealth. Never again would I be paid less than my male counterparts, nor silenced in the meetings he ran.

It is unfortunate that in all my years of pharmaceutical sales, my last position would result in the cowardice of a man who felt his power shrink in the fireworks-level notice of my efforts to others.

My earliest nudges to bring my sales and marketing intelligence to the world became a full-fledged kick in the ass to start my own dreams into reality. In these 2021-era early insights, I crafted for my umbrella company called Epizon Strategy Solutions. Epizon is the Greek word for survivor, and I have felt like a survivor for most of my fifty-five years on this earth.

Our first division is entitled Move Moment Atlas. Move Moment Atlas is a structured guide that helps digital marketers align their actions with their desired outcomes. The courses housed in MMA have become a blueprint for thousands of individuals seeking clarity in their business journey. At its core, Move Moment Atlas was about making calculated decisions in the digital marketing sphere while creating a foundation of security and protection, which would allow businesses to thrive without fear of uncontrolled outcomes created at the whims of others.

In the best use of time and talent, the individual's efforts held the momentum which could dictate the direction of efforts and success.

One of the most pivotal teachings I developed was the course called Braking Distance. Braking Distance has its origins in my world-wide work to eradicate the normalization of violence in a person's most intimate relationships. Much like I have trained over 100,000 people in corporations and individual efforts to create methods for safety in the workplace, I crafted Braking Distance as a space where we allow ourselves as digital entrepreneurs to step back, evaluate risks, and recalibrate our actions to ensure our digital marketing efforts remain secure and strategic. This approach was born from years of working with individuals who, despite their potential, often found themselves overwhelmed or vulnerable to the pitfalls of their most intimate relationships. Braking Distance took these personal insights, and created solutions for online business, whether through cyber threats, burnout, or misalignment in their objectives.

Through the course "Braking Distance: Protecting and Creating Your Safety in Your Digital Marketing Business," I teach entrepreneurs how to take control of their business environments. It is about understanding that not every opportunity should be pursued recklessly, and not every risk needs to be taken without careful evaluation. The key to empowering these moments was to create systems that prioritize both personal and professional protection, ensuring that growth does not come at the cost of well-being.

Next up, included a course on Eliminating Limiting Beliefs. As a trauma-informed certified coach, I've aimed to challenge the internal narratives that hold people back. Helping individuals dismantle these barriers has been a cornerstone of my teachings, allowing them to unlock their true potential. By creating a framework for removing self-imposed limitations, I've witnessed people experience breakthroughs, not only in their businesses but also in their personal lives.

By 2023, my work evolved into offering Changing Courses 11's Roadmap Exclusive as an affiliate program I would resell to any digital entrepreneur intent on learning the business or expanding their own portfolios. Roadmap Exclusive allows people who want to bring their personal passion into the digital world. My Mission, Vision, and Values closely mirrored Changing Courses 11's commitment for developing their own digital business with integrity and a commitment to developing a better experience for serving people in the online digital marketing world.

I knew I needed to find something like Roadmap Exclusive because of my own pitfalls and wasted money in digital marketing. My biggest downfall was my own experience of once paying an online digital coach $8000 to belong to her exclusive coaching community, only to find her promises hollow, and her follow through lacking in every way. When the second year sales pitch came to her current coaching fellowships via a weekend long planning session, I was excited to see what new things would come in year two.

Nothing.

In the world of fast-paced digital evolution there were no new offerings for this exclusive community with one glaring exception- a $7500 increase in the program to over $15,000 to stay with her coaching services.

There was no way my budget could take on $15,000 per year with a coach who was providing sub-par services to people desperate for help. Once I bowed out from year two, my personal learning portal with her was eliminated and my access withdrawn. The $8000 I paid didn't matter. All my learnings and courses were instantly removed and inaccessible to me. I realized that the $8000 I paid for one year of coaching was a complete waste of my time and money.

Last I checked in with this "guru" she was marketing her services away from the digital space and into teaching people who want to become national speakers. The same tired pitch deck from 2020 was being used, with only slight modifications related to speaking in front of an audience.

I knew I needed to craft solutions for digital marketing at a better price, and with access to all course offerings and teaching videos (with community support services) which would be forever accessible at one price for entry. It took me almost a year to find the integrity I demanded for my customers which was lacking in what I experienced in my own journey. My extensive networking in the digital marketing community brought me the insights that many people knew what they wanted but were unsure how to take the steps necessary to achieve those dreams.

Roadmap Exclusive became a step-by-step guide for turning visions into reality, helping individuals identify their purpose, eliminate distractions, and take action in meaningful ways. I am wildly proud to align myself with integrity, one low price for entry and life-long access to the course content (and any updates) at point of purchase.

Finally, the latest offering to my Move Moment portfolio is a sweet little (if little was the size of Texas) affiliate marketing partnership with a company called Cowboy Leisure. Cowboy Leisure takes digital marketing and brings the capability of effectively using Instagram Reels as a goldmine to crafting your brand and ensuring your customer message is not only seen, but making an impact. I am an affiliate marketer for Cowboy Leisure's product called "Reel Saloon" and it's for anyone who sells products on social media, in any industry, and any type of account. I know with the addition of Reel Saloon to my Move Moment portfolio we will be able to allow our customer family the best experience to use their own message to drive change.

The key to this entire Move Moment Atlas experience is built by fostering the awareness that every moment counts, and each action, when aligned with a purpose, can drive momentum toward success. Next, My Move Moment Atlas is designed for those pivotal points in time where we choose to take a step forward and propel us toward our wildest dreams. It's also meant to help eliminate the possible stalling when fear is present, but instead empower individuals to move beyond limiting beliefs and external distractions, refocusing on the actions that would bring their business and life closer to the realities they envisioned.

As I reflect on the past eight years, one of the most rewarding aspects of my journey has been seeing the transformations that take place when people truly commit to their own Move Moments. Empowerment, after all, is not just about achieving a single goal—it's about fostering sustainable growth, building lasting impact, and creating a ripple effect that touches not only the lives of business owners but also their customers, families, and communities.

Looking ahead, I envision a world where more people feel empowered to recognize and act on their Move Moments. In the digital age, where information is abundant and opportunities are limitless, the challenge isn't about having enough resources; it's about knowing how to navigate them effectively. This is where the teachings I've developed over the past eight years come into play.

I plan to continue evolving these concepts, ensuring that digital marketers, entrepreneurs, and individuals from all walks of life have the tools they need to protect their dreams, nurture their passions, and take decisive steps forward in their personal and professional journeys. In the years to come, I will expand on these frameworks, adding new layers of protection, empowerment, and strategy so that every Move Moment is seized with confidence and clarity.

Within Move Moment Atlas' design is the propensity to give back to people and community. It's a key part of our mission. This is where my commitment as the Founder and CEO of Safe In Harm's Way, will continue. I founded SafeInHarmsWay.org as an innovative nonprofit designed to support survivors of domestic violence through digital means. The organization, which is entirely online, offers resources that help survivors recognize and escape toxic relationships while fostering their emotional and physical healing. Safe In Harm's Way is built to meet survivors where they are, often in quiet, private moments when they are most vulnerable. Through a combination of storytelling, online resources, social media engagement, and a powerful network of volunteers, the organization helps survivors find support without alerting their abusers.

My vision for Safe In Harm's Way includes serving historically marginalized communities that face difficulties in accessing services due to economic, logistical, or awareness barriers. The organization provides trauma-informed resources that range from relationship advice to navigating the legal system, ensuring that help is available regardless of a survivor's situation. Our stealth approach to content delivery on social media allows users to discreetly access life-saving information. The organization's initiatives, including its emphasis on hashtags and volunteer follow-ups, have seen a significant increase in usage, highlighting the profound impact of their work

This pioneering approach has earned Safe In Harm's Way a reputation for being both innovative and deeply compassionate, giving survivors a path toward healing and empowerment at a person's fingertips. The latest focus on technology will catapult our service offerings to bring safety to every person impacted by violence.

Additionally, our professional training and policy consulting solutions will now focus on addressing domestic violence and its impact in the workplace and neighborhoods, by teaching friends, family, and coworkers how to be kind and thoughtful human connections for the people they know are navigating abuse. We have coupled these offerings with an incredible newly enhanced commitment to advocates working tirelessly in the domestic violence industry with low-cost solutions to their biggest dollar needs. The Safe In Harm's Way company mission will allow us to help all organizations mitigate the often hidden emotional and physical impacts of domestic violence on employees, which can significantly disrupt productivity, retention, and corporate culture. Our custom-tailored solution provides training and strategies for Fortune 500 companies, domestic violence shelters, and businesses across various industries to ensure that companies can both protect their workforce and enhance profitability through diversity, equity, and inclusion initiatives: with safety and mental health as primary drivers of success.

My life changes from 2016 have fueled my growth into dreams I never imagined, coming through in full technicolor glory for myself and the people I serve. With a focus on empowering individuals to achieve their wildest dreams by identifying and acting on professional expansion moments via Move Moment Atlas. My work emphasizes the importance of creating secure, sustainable, and growth-oriented business practices. This unique blend of strategic insight and personal development has inspired countless individuals to break free from limiting beliefs, protect their business endeavors, and align their actions with their deepest goals. And in a beautiful final moment of expansion our services at SafeInHarmsWay.org can expand to whole person community involvement which helps eliminate silence and shame, allowing for life-saving services to reach the people most in need.

Caroline Markel (formerly Markel-Hammond) is a four time international best selling author, public speaker, and CEO and Founder of both SafeInHarmsWay.org. and Epizon Strategy Solutions. Caroline's work with Fortune 500 corporations and billion-dollar brands has impacted 100,000 people to empower healing, and eliminate silence and shame. Over the past eight years, she has developed courses such as the **Move Moment Atlas**, designed to help individuals in the digital marketing space protect their dreams and achieve their wildest goals.

Through a focus on safety, empowerment, and community, Caroline has built a global network of support for digital entrepreneurs and domestic violence survivors alike.

Caroline's work is deeply rooted in her personal experiences, as she uses storytelling and advocacy to create change in the corporate and personal development world. Her results, showcased from Times Square to small town locations, lead to individualized and uniquely-designed healing solutions which foster confidence, safety, privacy, and build community.

As a trauma-informed coach, and 20 Most Inspiring Leader, Caroline's personal journey of navigating the "after" of human crime and violence has been featured on Oprah, Forbes, PBS, NPR, Ms. Magazine, Newsweek, television, radio and podcasts. Her team's efforts have included numerous awards, including two Manny Awards and four Anthem Awards.

Caroline can be found leading the charge in disrupting complacency and fostering growth. Through her initiatives, Caroline is committed to ensuring that every individual has the tools and support needed to thrive. She can be found anywhere across the globe, coupling her advocacy with travel for live music and creating intimate gatherings for chosen family and friends.

Discover Caroline's Full Line of Course Offerings and Solutions to Create Your Own Dreams Here. https://stan.store/movemomentatlas
Resources:

Move Moment Atlas: https://stan.store/movemomentatlas
CarolineMarkel.com: https://carolinemarkel.com/
LinkedIn: Caroline Markel: https://www.linkedin.com/in/carolinemarkel/
LinedIn: Epizon Strategy: https://www.linkcdin.com/company/epizon-strategy-solutions/
LinkedIn: Safe In Harm's Way: https://www.linkedin.com/company/safe-in-harms-way/
Caroline Markel on Spotify:
https://open.spotify.com/user/31vpbnk5jlob4cg5xgzqekk6uxcu/playlists
Eliminating Limiting Beliefs on Spotify:
https://open.spotify.com/playlist/6lQRVSFVoWcTZdm7xgkWuM?si=9edbf21356f34459
Caroline Markel on Facebook:
https://www.facebook.com/CarolineMarkelPublic/
Caroline Markel on
Instagram:https://www.instagram.com/thecarolinemarkel/
Move Moment Atlas on Instagram: @movemomentatlas

LITTLE BELLIES

I would try to shrink as small as I could as I walked back to my seat at the back of the class holding my blue punch card in my hand. I felt like everyone was watching me and they knew. They knew we didn't live in a big house. They knew we drove an older car. They knew we were poor because I had the BLUE ticket, not the green one.

I got free lunch at school, and I was so embarrassed.

On the other side of this was a mom. MY mom. A mom that knew that even though she had to leave quickly while her violently abusive husband was away, her children would get a meal at school while she took the steps to become financially independent.

As a child all I felt was embarrassment. Now, a mom myself, I needed that help in 2013 when I lost my husband to severe asthma. Through these lenses, all I see is gratitude.

So many women have to stay in dangerous situations because of financial abuse. My mother was one of them. She was a stay-at-home mom when my younger brother and sister came along, and she did all the things a kid would love about having a parent home. Reading together, playing together, bandaging up scraped knees and elbows. Cooking, oh the meals my mom would make. Homemade bread and cookies. I remember the first time I ate a homemade doughnut. It was a weekend morning, and my mom had a big pot of oil on the stove. I watched as she cut out circles and then little holes into the circles. Then she fried them until they were golden brown. They were so good. Warm vanilla cake doughnuts. No added glaze. No sugar dusting. To this day I love the plain doughnuts at Dunkin Donuts and grocery stores because they remind me of that morning.

But those mornings were the sunshine that came after really dark nights. My brother and sister's father was nothing short of a monster. There was no abuse box he didn't tick but the worst one was making sure mom never had enough money to leave. We had everything we needed and more. He provided a good life financially. The rest of everything else he provided was terrifying.

My mom did what she was "supposed to" and told her friends, family members and neighbors. Back then, few people wanted to "get involved" in a dangerous situation. Some would listen and just tell her they were so sorry. Some would tell a story of their own and some just didn't care. Then she found that person that was ready to take action and knew how to find some resources and they did the homework together. Making calls, hunting down resources and creating an escape plan.

The day we left was a whirlwind. I remember staying at her amazing friend's house and then transitioning into a new apartment complex with big yards and lots of mom neighbors with kids. I remember making friends there within days. I remember feeling SAFE. I remember Santa actually visited us that year with presents. A big black sack of them and my mom crying. I was too old to believe but didn't understand the enormity of this at the time either. Her story had made it to the hospital surgical ward, and they helped her provide a Christmas morning for us to celebrate as our new family. I watched my mom start to have moments of joy. She built friendships with some amazing women while we were there. A few remained in her life for years after we left the complex.

I also remember NOT being hungry. I remember eating meals we had never had before like breakfast sausage with egg noodles, peas and applesauce. Kraft macaroni and cheese with fish sticks and homemade tartar sauce. Hotdogs with tater tots and one of my favorites, that I just made tonight, that we call pasta, tomato and cheese. Cooked medium shell pasta, broken up stewed tomatoes in their juice and cut up medium cheddar cheese, baked in the oven and topped with salt and pepper. The flavors now remind me of those days, and I crave them a couple times a year. My brother, sister and I all remember this as one of our favorites.

My mother was strong, proud and determined. Strong in that, she knew when she needed to ask for help. We benefited from free lunch, food banks and the government food program. (that big block of cheese was so good) Proud to take those years and go back to school and become a successful business owner with her own salon. Determined to make sure that we had a roof over our heads, food in our bellies and taught us we needed to work for what we wanted.

She taught us not to keep secrets and to always put our health and safety first because those are our biggest treasures. When I share my story with other women, I realize how big this one sentence is...*I also remember NOT being hungry.* I hear from many my age how "proud" their parents were that they would not accept help in the food department. I have come to see over the past decade how deep the shame is in regard to food insecurity and there is no need for that shame. No need for a hungry belly if you are in an area that has resources. Food pantries, EBT programs, WIC, generous neighbors. Help doesn't always scream it's available but when the wrong side of pride is put aside and you ask, it is there. Just be PROUD enough to know you are WORTH the help. My mission is to normalize asking for help with food when it's needed. My books and podcast were created to allow fundraising for Maine's largest food bank. Good Shepherd Food Bank, they help over 600 pantries at a local level and donated dollars are matched by local corporations.

I take PRIDE in being raised by a woman who escaped a monster and showed me that nothing is impossible if you are willing to work, find resources, make change and be a good human. You don't need to start your own non-profit to make a BIG change. Find one near you that you are passionate about and help them. My mother is now retired but is always helping the non-profit she is passionate about, Angel's Wing. And in the update, we all seem to want on social media, I'll tell you here, she beat breast cancer in the past year and just celebrated her 29th anniversary with an amazing man I am happy to call my Dad. ❤

Melissa Mansfield-Anderson
CEO Mansfield Anderson Publishing
Founder A Moose Bush Podcast/Book Series

She is a 3-time best-selling author, national speaker on women's empowerment and a passionate fighter against childhood hunger. Melissa has been working for years, with women to tell and publish their stories to help heal the world one survivor at a time. Now she uses her experience and love of the food and beverage industry to create projects that can raise funds for the leading non-profit in Maine. Good Shepherd Food Bank services over 600 food pantries across the state, making sure that the food insecure have a resource to help feed their families.

Melissa is currently working on a new restaurant finder app, Chomp207.com, for local foodies. The app will connect prospective diners with the flavors, atmosphere and experiences they are looking for while collaborating with restaurants to increase funds and resources for the food insecure.

You can connect with Melissa through social media or through her website.
www.amoosebush.com
www.mansfieldanderson.com
facebook.com/BeTheChangeYouWish2CInTheWorld

I DIDN'T CHOOSE THIS LIFE

Why should you read this story? My editor keeps throwing this question at me, and it's hard to answer. In its most simple form, the story is about my son. I want people to know my son. What he stands for, and his positive impact in the world. I also never want to forget my son, for anyone that had the pleasure of knowing my son, or all the people that didn't know my son- to never forget him. My writing effort is as much for me, as it is for this book.

I am also supposed to write about me, and why I made the choices I did. I have to admit that while I love my editor, she is also annoying. But I'm trying. Golly, I'm trying.

I'd love for any person to read this, and at a time when the world seems overwhelming, remember that the choices you make in life matter. Kindness matters. Inclusion matters. Being your authentic self matters. Not judging people matters.

Offering forgiveness matters. Realize that holding grudges doesn't take away pain, it only expands pain to a deeper level. It's always easy to stumble upon pain; especially on a random Monday, and have it change your life forever.

So, I hope you join me on the lessons, and you read through to the end. I hope this makes you think about the world a little differently.

Most importantly, I hope you look at your children as absolute intelligent and kind people with their own wants, needs, dreams, and ideas. Listen to them and be open to their friends in your home. And I mean really listen; not look up from your phone and nod but be present and engage.

This story was written in 2023, but actually I'd like to introduce you to Tanner Ryan Lewis, aka Bear, circa 2016.

To be specific, February of 2016.

An exact day? Monday, February 1st, 2016.

These are the first flashbacks I have of ***that*** evening.

I had started a new job, with a short commute. When I arrived home, my best friend Mike asked if he could come over, make dinner, and have a game night. Sounded perfect to me!! Mike came over and fixed a great chicken dinner with sides and salads. I'm still spoiled when it comes to my bff, Mike.

As we were sitting on my living room floor, eating dinner and playing backgammon, it felt like we were living our best lives.

And then the doorbell rang.

I didn't really budge. I don't like surprises and unexpected visitors, so I was just going to ignore the doorbell, and carry on with our dinner and game.

Then the pounding started. A loud and consistent pounding on the door.

I started to panic, so I sent Mike to check out the commotion. Mike peeked out the window and said, "It's the cops."

I freaked out and started to sneak down the hallway to hide. I mean, what was I supposed to do? None of what was happening made any sense to me. None.

Mike peeked out the window again, and his face is forever etched in my mind and my heart. The color literally drained from his face, and he turned white. "Hayley, we HAVE to answer the door, there is someone with the officers."

The rest is a blur.

Can you imagine standing in something familiar like your own home, but nothing coming out of a stranger's mouth makes sense, even though you understand the words being said? And the words are coming at you, but you're physically trying to duck down, because the words feel violent. In fact, these words could accidentally kill you. Or your son. Or his friend.

The words I am dodging all made sense, because I knew the people mentioned, and I could grasp that there was a problem. But my gosh, I am drowning in confusion from these words because giving in to understanding them would mean something I could not ever live with again. It would mean that I would be living a life I never chose.

It would mean I would suddenly and forever be living without my Bear. My Tanner. My son.

So the words are flashing around me, and leaving a trail of understanding, but not understanding at all. BOOM! Words like flash bulbs popping in my face, as I stand in my living room listening to strangers speak.

Accident.
    Nathan.
    Lynn.
    Tanner.
    Gone.

Wait. Tanner is still alive?
    Must go fast to the hospital.
    Pryor Road.
    Less than 2 miles from our home.
    Still hope.

What do I want to do right now at this very moment? Have Mike please make these people leave. I wanted to collapse, and so I did. I tried pushing Sargeant Evans out of my home; our home, as if getting him to leave, meant none of this was happening. I know I punched him in his huge, black, bullet proof vest, and begged him to just GO AWAY.

I mean, c'mon! We were having such a fun and relaxing Monday night. Why is there even a Sergeant Evens talking to me right now? Repeatedly. Over and over. I asked Mike to please make them go away.

Instead, Mike looked blankly at me and said, "Hayley- we need to go find Tanner, get your shoes".

Here are the random things your brain does in insane moments which are incomprehensible. Your beautiful brain creates distractions to everything happening. This is done, so that you don't need to pay attention to everything happening.

But it's all trickery. Because then the brain decides, without your knowledge or consent, to let loose of distractions in the form of remembering random moments. And then again, BOOM! Your brain shuts down, so that you can remember nothing.

It's like thunderstorm flashes of lightning, when there is no rain. But then the downpour starts, and you can remember every drop, and how the grass smells in the rain, and exactly how many inches of rain fell, plus who was standing next to you holding an umbrella. Oh wait! Wait, because just as quickly, the rain stops in an immediate absence of sound, and you're left with only silence and reverberating echoes of words being said, and they have no meaning to you any longer- even if you've been saying them for years.

Let me offer you the random memories of my brain, because I can still feel and smell them as strongly as I cannot remember absolutely key moments. .

I remember following the police car to CenterPoint Hospital.

I remember making a few phone calls on the way. I remember calling my daughter Sierra, just a few years younger than her brother, Tanner. I remember Sierra was one of the first people to know, via social media.

Apparently, people were talking about 3 boys in an accident on Pryor Road. I remember calling my Mom, although I have zero memory of any words we exchanged.

I remember calling my Dad in California. I remember his screech-scream, "NOOOOOOOOOOOOOOOOO." My dad's guttural cry will haunt me for the rest of my life. I will never get that out of my mind. Never, not ever. I can still hear it. Daily.

I remember arriving at the hospital, and it was filled with so many people I knew.

I remember looking for Sierra? I wanted to grab Sierra, hold her, and never let her leave my sight.

My former husband Benjamin was there, of course. Benjamin is the only true Dad Tanner ever had. Benjamin had a couple friends with him, and I remember thinking it was great to see them, and have their love and support.

I remember an exhale. (And probably the last time I fully exhaled in peace again. Ever. Still.)

Tanner is dead.
Tanner is dead.
Tanner is dead.

And now, after arriving, the staff wants to know if I want to see him. I was so confused. I didn't know. I didn't want to have any regrets either way, but how can I be expected to make that choice so soon? I trust Benjamin. He's the smartest person I know, very levelheaded, and always makes the right decision. Benjamin said we shouldn't see him. I am forever grateful that he said no. I have no regrets.

Except for not asking for a lock of Tanner's hair.

My Mom wanted to go see Tanner. I remember asking her to please not go. I didn't want my Mom to be haunted, and to have him dead as her last image. But if you know my Mom, she knows what she wants, and doesn't let anything get in her way. (She's the second smartest person I know).

I know it was at least a year before I had the courage to ask her what Tanner looked like. She answered in one word, "Peaceful."

I remember the ER people asking me if I wanted to take home his clothing. I don't know what he wore that day, for my last memory of him was peeking in his room at 6am that Monday morning before I left for work. He was in bed sleeping. I patted his head and said, "I love you Bear" as I did every morning before I left. I didn't want his dead clothes. At all.

Golly! I really wish that I had asked for a lock of his hair. He had the best hair.

But where was my mind? Not present at all. I don't remember the drive home at all. Nothing.

I received a call from Midwest Organ Donor on 2.2.2016, the day after he died. We had a two-hour conversation about Tanner, his health, his wishes, his lifestyle, blah blah blah. Two hours. I know it's necessary because his driver's license clearly stated he's an organ donor, and I know organs have a lifespan. So, I muscled through the call for Tanner. That's what he wanted. (Side note: Midwest Organ Donor is a great company with very compassionate people. Maybe think about following Tanner's wishes and sign up to be an organ donor.)

Planning for his service? Hardly remember. I think I was there with my Mom, Benjamin, and his wife Jen. The whole funeral biz is so weird to me. Profiting by people that are NOT in their right mind to be making decisions when they are consumed by a grief fog. Tanner wanted to be cremated, so we didn't have to pick out the box or whatever, but still ended up costing $8k.

Day of service? I remember what I wore because I still wear the same dress on every Mother's Day; or anything that has to do with Tanner. My peacock dress.

I remember flowers. A lot. Too many.

I remember being dizzy for standing so long, because the line was NEVER ending. I remember Mike physically holding me up at times. I couldn't take a break. I remember being thankful that all of Sia's cheer team came to support her. I remember them being girls, and trying to pretend they weren't where they were, and for what reason.

Sierra's brother was dead. In all their short thirteen years together, they never fought once. And now her best friend was gone.

I remember the funeral people gloating to me about the "turnout", and how they can't believe how many people were there- "might be our record". They were proud and smiling. I was pissed. I remember saying to him, "Okay, so frame a picture and I'll sign it for you". Assholes.

I remember dividing up all the flower arrangements. I don't have any idea how they got to my home, but they did. I remember Tanner's "Baby Mama" (our inside joke) Tresa, taking photos of EVERY flower arrangement so I had pictures to remember, since flowers don't last forever.

That's pretty much where memory stops again.

I do remember the first moment I discovered my new Superpower. I do remember one co-worker who I didn't really have a reason to interact with (different department) coming up to me. Cheryl approached me at work. It's at this moment that my new "skills" came over me. I could see it in her eyes IMMEDIATELY. She's a bereaved Mom too. She lost her son, Brian. As time passes, I can easily spot another bereaved parent. In an instant. A special gift I wouldn't wish upon anyone. Cheryl reached out without really knowing me, at a time when I needed it most. We are still friends to this day, even after having left the job. It's a good lesson to remember that breaking silence means you can lessen shame and despair and accept strength and love when not expected.

I remember a lot of questions from everyone I encountered. And those questions were all about FORGIVENESS.

Tanner's friend, Collin, was driving the car with Tanner and their friend, Nathan.

Collin is 1000% responsible for killing my child, and killing Nathan, too.

Forgiveness wasn't ever a question for me. I've never blamed Collin in any way. I know our kids. Who had the most gas on that day was the metric on which they chose who would drive. It was their daily routine after school.

Nathan's truck was parked in front of my house when I got home from work on February 1, 2016. Tanner's car was in our driveway. Process of elimination- Collin must have had the most gas.

It could have been ANY ONE of those three boys that was the driver. Did Colin make a TERRIBLE driving decision that day? Absolutely. In the blink of an eye- one bad decision. I've read the police report hundreds of times, and the eyewitnesses' descriptions of the crash. Heart wrenching and makes me sick. Questions haunt me daily- did it all happen in slow motion? Did Tanner and Nate see the car heading straight for them, when Collin's car was fishtailing? Were they scared? Were they screaming? I'll never be able to have those questions answered. One thought, however, that puts my mind at peace, is that they died happy. They died together, doing what they loved- heading to "B Dub" as they did every day after school. Together.

The accident put Collin into a coma, and again we are back to a key moment that I have no memory of; I have no idea for how long Collin remained unconscious. I do recall Colin's mom, Jolene, telling me his first question when he woke up. He said, "Please tell me Tanner is okay."

Jolene had to say, "No."

Collin had nothing in his system, besides his prescribed medication for depression/anxiety. I still to this day dislike people jumping to conclusions about three 18-year-old boys in a car accident, and how they must have been drunk or high. Nope. All of them were clean and sober that February 1st day.

Collin's choices forced him to now face three felony charges. Two for the deaths of Nathan and Tanner, and one for assault on the other driver. The other driver luckily walked away without physical injury- but I'm sure he struggles knowing his vehicle smashed into another and killed two kids.

I attended every court hearing that Collin had to face.

I fought for Collin's freedom. I testified on his behalf. It was hard. Unthinkably hard.

Collin knows his actions killed his two best friends, and his actions were entirely PREVENTABLE.

On the day of sentencing, Collin wore a peacock tie for Tanner. as that was our symbol. At sentencing, after all victim impact pleas for Collin, he was sentenced to the minimum of 21 years. TWENTY-ONE YEARS. Seven years per felony.

I lost it in the courtroom. I ran out and puked. Lynn (Nathan's Mom) grabbed me, and said that's just the sentence. She fully believed Collin would get out for good behavior.

Collin wrote me a letter almost every other day while he was in jail. He was scared. He was very well behaved and polite (duh- all of my bonus kids are), and he was released after 4 months. Thank gosh.

And now, as I write this, thinking about Collin wearing a peacock tie, I am remembering how peacocks entered our world.

Before his death, Tanner and I were considering matching tattoos. Tanner had typed out a novel about why he was old enough, and mature enough, to decide what his first tattoo would be. He researched what tattoo would symbolize our relationship. Tanner explained in a letter to me what the peacock symbolizes. I read his words over and over.

Everything Tanner did, he did to the fullest.

Tanner, Sierra, and I had a vacation planned to Hermosa Beach, CA to get these matching peacock tattoos. Tanner wanted to take the train to California and had done all the homework for which tattoo shop to use. 3rd Street Tattoo was chosen, and Tanner even had our appointments scheduled. I still have the texts from the morning of February 1, 2016, sharing our peacock tattoo ideas- he was so excited to get his FIRST tattoo.

But Tanner died. He died before the trip. He died before his first tattoo.

So what were Sierra and I to do? As the day of the trip approached, Sierra didn't want to go anymore. Understandable. She lost her one and only sibling. She lost her big brother. She lost her best friend.

Enter my best friend Mike again, who wanted to go in Tanner's spot. I asked Mike if we could at least fly. Nope. Tanner wanted to take the train, Tanner had already purchased our train tickets, and that's what we're going to do. So, we did. Kansas City to Los Angeles on a train is NOT QUICK!

This trip is a blur to me. I know we took a lot of pictures, and we made a lot of memories. I wore sunglasses the entire time to hide the constant tears. Mike and I both got peacock tattoos for Tanner, and even had his ashes put in the ink.

As time goes on, the remaining friends start living their own lives of marriage, kids, and LIFE. My timeline stopped at age 18. It's hard for me emotionally to see them being real life adults. But I know their lives go on.

But there was still one more tragic outcome to be experienced from February 1, 2016.

Tanner was always worried about Collin's use of drugs, and came to me often asking what he can do to help him. I never had an answer. No one does. Collin succumbed to his addiction. In my heart, I know it wasn't intentional. But I don't know a lot about drug use and differentiating between suicide or accidental overdose. I know in my heart he would never leave me, his Mom or his friends- ever. So that's what I choose to think. Collin died of an accidental overdose.

So now, three families are entirely destroyed again- by this one stupid driving decision that was so preventable. Collin was buried wearing his peacock tie, and I placed one of Tanner and Nathan's wristbands on his chest.

Tanner, Nathan, and Collin leave behind the most genuine group of young adults that one would ever be lucky enough to know. If I've said it once, I've said it a million times- I find myself literally shaking my head in disbelief of their kindness, and the adults they've become.

Never fake- ever. Genuine as can be. Who raised these kids?? Oh wait, we all did. Together.

As a family that was attempted to be destroyed by this incident (not an accident, it was an incident). These young men and women are a beautiful rainbow from Hispanic, to black, to hippy, to Iranian, to white. But every single one would take a bullet for the other. Very old souls, and those who knew even one of the bros, is a better person for it. And they're all my kids.

My son. Tanner. He taught me so much in his fast 18.65 years. And it's a lesson for anyone to take away from these tragedies. Be yourself. Be your audacious self, and pursue what makes you happy. Because when you do, you surround yourself with other people who live their own lives, regardless of race, sex, or religion.

How did Tanner live his life? He never met a stranger. He adored babies, animals and elderly all the same. He was the statement maker when it came to style and thought outside the box. I worried about him and his style on occasion. But when he died, I learned his friends were envious of his confidence. He shopped at thrift stores, and he pegged his jeans. He lived how HE wanted to live.

Me, as his Mom was always worried about him being bullied. But Tanner didn't care, and of course, was never bullied. Tanner was a leader. A trend setter. A positive influencer. His friends had access to his clothing (after he died), shoe collection, sock collection (yes- he loved his socks), and his girlfriend, Aubrey, had access to his boxer collection. Every single friend had an item or two of his that brought back memories.

Prom of 2017? The bros wore his Vans and socks- many of them. Beautiful photos, and glad they took Tanner to their Senior Prom.

He was the kid that would sit with anyone at lunch who was eating alone. He was the one that would give his last dollar to anyone at the vending machine to get a snack. He was the one that had the idea to go to Walgreens and put together dozens of bags to keep in the car for whenever we came upon homeless people; even thinking to buy feminine products for any females we encountered.

He was the kid- when he caught me secretly crying about finances… would come to me and say, "Mom- it's just the water bill. No big deal. Let's go play frisbee." He'd go outside, ready to play frisbee together. Me? I'd literally fall to my knees, wipe my tears, then head to the backyard to throw the disc.

He played every sport, even attempted football one year. As Tanner ran next to his teammate carrying the ball, cheering him on, Benjamin and I decided maybe football wasn't the sport for him. Baseball? Best catcher for years, and so good, too. Basketball? Scrappy because of his height but made his high school team. He played in the high school orchestra, too. Cello, then bass.

Tanner did it all. Lacrosse was super fun to watch and learn about that sport. Golf? Of course he loved golf. He had his Dad, Benjamin, to learn from and play with. Fondest memories of spying on them in the garage together. Whether polishing up golf clubs or oiling up their ball gloves- rubber bands and all, they were a magical pair.

Music was a deep connection for me and Tanner; something that bonded Tanner and I together regardless of artist or genre. We didn't agree on everything but had a lot in common as well. Lyrics? This is what the bros were all about. So deep and didn't just listen to the music, they LISTENED to the music. Tanner would often come to me and ask me to listen to a song. Really LISTEN.

Doesn't matter if it's Bob Marley, Grateful Dead, Mac Miller, Logic...... Listen to the words. Our best conversations were discussing lyrics. He was not a Dave Matthews fan like his Mom. Not at all. (I only dragged him to one show- unforgettable memories about that show- another day!). But he came to me one day in 2015 and said, "Mom- I just listened to this song and I really appreciate and understand the lyrics- I dig it!" I was floored. So proud. Song was "Two Step", by Dave Matthews.

Walking away today, after reading this chapter, please take away the lyric Tanner loved so much from Two Step:

Celebrate we will
'Cause life is short but sweet for certain
(Hey)
We climb on two by two
To be sure these days continue
Things we cannot change
Things we cannot change

Life can change in an instant, and that instant can last forever. So, in the meantime, love hard. Be inclusive of everyone. Worry about your friends and worry about the homeless. Try everything once and keep trying new experiences regardless of age.

I am also going to throw in to act with compassion. I use the services of The Compassionate Friends as a community of people who have lost children way before their time. But you can be compassionate in real life, too. If you know someone who has lost a child, or someone who has lived through extreme trauma, realize that the brain can take a long time to heal, if ever. Forgetfulness is common, and so is a hyper focus. Love people through forgetfulness and hyper-focus, regardless of time and space needed to heal.

Finally, choose forgiveness as often as you can. I can't imagine what it would feel like for me to have held a grudge against Collin, only to lose him, too. Apologize and offer forgiveness. Repeatedly.

Rest in Paradise, my sons.

Tanner
June 19, 1997- February 1, 2016
Nathan
October 10, 1997- February 1, 2016
Collin
September 10, 1997- August 22, 2020

You are all loved beyond measure, and the "special cargo" on every drive. (Nathan's quote every time he drove my Tanner).

Hayley Lewis is a best-selling author, accountant extraordinaire, and "Mom" to Tanner and Sierra. As the main architect in designing her own life, Hayley can be found digging a variety of businesses out of their bookkeeping and accounting errors. It's the business acumen which corporations pursue for her sought-after intelligence, but it's the people skills and authentic investment in others that make her a welcome addition to every team. Hayley's skills also extend into event planning, ensuring every element of a large or small corporate, nonprofit, and personal events are curated to every guest's expectation.

After losing her son, Tanner, in a car accident, Hayley committed to keeping him alive with connections to his chosen family of friends, and the Compassionate Friends community across the United States. She hopes to one day continue her high school-aged focus, which had been in collaboration with Collin (the driver in Tanner's car accident) before Collin's death. Their original goal was to speak about teen driving, safety and overall "we're invincible" attitude. Besides discussing teen driving, defensive driving and general safety reminders, Hayley commits to discussing traits that are important to emotional wellbeing, like forgiveness, handling grief, and communication between peers. She will always be navigating day by day, for it's not the expected path she thought would be for her.

It's this same commitment to friends-as-family which is evident in her love language of nicknames and being the first to ask, "How can I help?", and is available to talk to any of Tanner's friends and family members anytime, for she feels no one should endure this unfortunate journey alone.

Whether driving her convertible (top down, and wind blowing in her hair, of course) or traveling around the world to see the Dave Matthews Band, Hayley keeps her schedule full with following Sierra's competitive cheer team competitions Nationwide. Hayley also loves giving back with volunteering hours and is the first to volunteer. Majority of her "empty nest" free hours are spent especially for marginalized or at-risk women and children, her passion for shelter animals, and much needed work at local Kansas City homeless shelters.

Discover Hayley's in-depth musings on Facebook or online at: neverchosethislife.com

SYSTEMIC CHANGE FOR SURVIVORS OF DOMESTIC VIOLENCE: YELLING FROM THE ROOFTOPS TOGETHER

I always knew I wanted to work with kids. Kids are carefree and fun. Honest. Resilient. As a younger adult I was a gymnastics and cheerleading coach, able to have a team of kids that I was able to lead in a positive way and through connection. My kids taught me more about life than I had ever learned in school and through these experiences, it cemented my plans to go to graduate school to become a child and family therapist.

As a young clinician in the field, I assumed that I would work with children who experienced anxiety and depression, struggles in school, having a difficult time transitioning after divorce, and other common struggles of childhood. For a while I thought I would specialize in working with eating disorders, but that lasted just a few years. I was naive; I knew I would run into child abuse and neglect and other childhood traumas, but I believed it would be infrequent. I believed that our world was safe based on the one I grew up in. Over time, though, I learned that for many children, this was not the case. That it was far more common than I could ever imagine.

As a young clinician in the field, I worked with children in several different settings. I worked at a children's hospital in the inpatient eating disorder unit, at an agency that contracted with Child Protective Services (CPS), and soon after having my first child, I started a private practice in my community. In each of these settings, there was a dynamic that I couldn't put my finger on and wasn't trained to identify in so many of my cases. The dynamic...was domestic violence and coercive control.

I am not actually sure when I was first able to name it. I think it was as I worked in the agency and had domestic violence on the reports we received from CPS as to why we were going to be involved with a family. Now, even though I had this language and reason for why I would be going into a family's home to do therapy with the children and caregivers to work towards creating safety in the home, I really had no idea what it meant. You see, in my graduate program (and in most graduate programs for counseling), domestic violence and coercive control are not taught about. I remember having a short discussion, maybe 30 minutes long, in a family issues class about this. What did I get out of that discussion? "If there is domestic violence, don't do couples work." While this small piece of knowledge is absolutely correct, I had no idea what to look for, or how to assess and treat those impacted by domestic violence. I still believed the misconceptions that are prevalent in our society today; that domestic violence was about physical violence, that all victims were young, uneducated women with low socioeconomic standing, that there were programs that would help these women leave, and that this was enough.

So, it was an interesting thing when caseworkers deemed me as "good at working with DV." What did that even mean? What was I doing?

Unfortunately, my supervisors did not know much more about it than I did, and so I stumbled along, making many mistakes along the way. I know now that some of those mistakes likely caused harm. At the time, I had no idea.

Fast forward to a year or so into my private practice. I was still getting referral after referral from the county CPS and from our local advocacy agency for child and adult survivors of domestic violence. There were things that I still could not understand. "Why would someone continue going back to their abuser?" "Why would they allow orders of protection to be broken?" "Why the heck wasn't our system doing more to support these families?" "Why were none of the abusers being held accountable?" And so, I started to really dive deep. I picked up every book I could read. I reached out to schedule time with the domestic violence advocates. I asked other therapists during consultation groups. But mostly, I really started to study and learn from my clients.

And while this was a huge turning point and time of growth in my life, the real change happened when I was called over and over to testify in family court for several of my child clients and heard the stories of family court from my adult survivor clients. It seemed like no one in a position of power was doing anything to keep my kids safe. In fact, they were being put in harm's way on a regular basis. I learned that a "high conflict" divorce was actually a term for abuse. And I learned that this belief I had that our systems would do what was in a child's best interest was untrue. What the actual F*ck!

Now that I knew, I could not sit idly by and let this continue. I started speaking out on any platform that I thought would make a difference. Very often I felt defeated. It seemed like everyone wanted to keep things status quo and look the other way. The realization that the person serving you in a restaurant, cleaning your teeth, or teaching your children could be a victim seems too much for many. This idea that anyone, no matter your level of education, ethnicity, or financial situation, could become a victim is too scary to hold on to.

I began creating content to train other mental health professionals. I wrote an e-book on what clinicians need to know to support survivors and not cause harm in the process. I started creating content on social media platforms to get the word out and to find connections to others who were passionate about bringing awareness to this cause and population. It was on LinkedIn when I finally found my people. I started connecting with an advocate here and a mental health professional there, and when the connections began, the collaboration started to happen. I started to see that I wasn't a lone wolf speaking out into a void. This only allowed me to become louder.

An unfortunate realization on my journey was that the misconceptions about domestic violence and lack of understanding of coercive control runs extremely deep, even amongst mental health professionals. I often heard, "well, I don't really work with victims of domestic violence in my practice," as a reason to not engage or get training. While initially I fought tooth and nail to get them to see that if they had 20 adult female clients, then it was likely that 5 were or would be victims (about 3 if they were male clients), eventually I decided to shift my focus a bit.

While I still train mental health professionals, I decided to focus on what I have seen to be the most important aspect of healing from abuse and accelerating the healing process exponentially for survivors, finding safe connections and community. A place where there are others who have experienced similar trauma. A place where a survivor can speak without having to constantly defend themselves. A place where the professionals leading have done the work to understand what abuse looks like while in the relationship as well as what it looks like after someone leaves.

In late 2021, I started *Rising Beyond Power and Control, The Rising Beyond Community*, and a year later, *The Rising Beyond Podcast*. It is in these places I have the opportunity to offer hope, support, and a place for survivors to heal. We offer resources, live online groups and Q&A sessions, online courses, and a safe, online forum where survivors can connect and get support from their fellow community members. Knowing that not everyone has the financial or time accessibility to join our community or that a group setting feels extremely vulnerable and dangerous, I decided to start *The Rising Beyond Podcast*. I get to shout from the rooftops to anyone who needs support and to professionals working with survivors about everything I have learned in the last decade of this work. I get to allow survivors to share their stories of abuse and recovery. I get to offer validation to those who I may never meet.

What about my passion for working with children? Yep, I am still doing that. In my private practice, that is, which has now grown to 7 clinicians and offers a training program for master's level interns, and still specializes in working with children. I have the privilege to train my clinicians in what I was never trained in as a young clinician. And, by helping protective parents heal, I have a greater impact on children than I ever could by working with a child individually.

I have also become active to create systemic change, connecting with legislators in Colorado to start tackling this enormous problem of post separation abuse through the family court system and the lack of attention and care our children's rights are given during this process. At the time of this writing, Kayden's Law was just passed in Colorado. The first of its kind, with the goal of increasing the education of professionals involved in the family court system, preventing uneducated and biased experts from testifying in these cases, and preventing children from being removed from a protective parent to improve the relationship with an abusive parent.

Over the years, it has felt like no one was listening or that nobody cared. This is not true. There are some that want to turn away, and when I was trying to create change in a silo, by myself, the goal seemed near impossible. But, when I became connected with others passionate about this space, passionate about sharing the voices of those without a voice, the goal became in our reach.

Quotes:

"There is an inverse relationship between shame and self-forgiveness. As you begin to forgive yourself, your shame will start to leave you."

"If you have privilege in any way, shape or form, find your way to use it for those without it."

"When you are healing from the isolation and destruction done by an abusive partner, it is important to put people around you who will mirror back the amazing qualities that make up who you are. When you can see yourself the way they see you, you will start to see yourself that way too."

Affirmations:

"I serve, I deserve."

"I am clear on my boundaries, and I will respond accordingly."

"I do not need permission for how I live my life."

"I am proud of my progress and will reach my goal in time."

Sybil is a Licensed professional Counselor and Approved Clinical Supervisor specializing in working with victims and survivors of narcissistic abuse and domestic violence, including the youngest witnesses. She owns a small group therapy practice in Colorado and after witnessing the constant ethical issues survivors experience in the family court system trying to protect their children, she also started Rising Beyond Power and Control to support survivors dealing with post separation abuse. Sybil also started The Rising Beyond Podcast to offer support to a larger audience in 2022 and is active in legislative changes in Colorado.

Links:

https://www.risingbeyondpc.com/

https://therisingbeyondpodcast.buzzsprout.com/share

https://www.linkedin.com/in/sybil-cummin-lpc-acs-50537791/
https://www.instagram.com/risingbeyondpc

https://www.facebook.com/risingbeyondpowerandcontrol

https://www.youtube.com/@beyondpowerandcontrol8485

EMBRACING THE UNKNOWN

"Are you sitting down?" I heard the doctor ask on the other end of the phone. It was one of those movie-like moments that takes your breath away. The kind where the light flashes and goes blank instantly before your eyes. It was a moment I never saw coming at 29 years old.

A few days earlier I'd gone into her office for a biopsy after a routine pelvic exam turned dark. The day after my exam, the nurse called me to tell me that a "scary" inconsistency came back on my pap smear, and they needed to get me in "right away."

While I never imagined what would strike me as my life flashing before my eyes on that call that day, I remember sitting on the exam table waiting for the biopsy days before, and I knew. With my whole body, I knew something was wrong. I just didn't know what it was.

I wept during the appointment as the gynecologist I'd only seen for the first time during the pelvic appointment and now the biopsy appointment said, "We just don't know." in a condescending tone. I wept when she called to confirm what my gut had seemingly already told me on that table. I had cervical cancer.

The diagnosis came on September 8, 2014. Looking back now there were subtle signs. In the summer months before, I'd felt exhausted most days. One Monday after executing a mountainside wedding for my side wedding planning business over the weekend, I'd come down with shingles that lasted for several weeks. Earlier in the year, I'd had a rash on my leg that, despite my best efforts, wouldn't go away no matter what I tried.

I chalked it all up to a busy life and career. I was, after all, running a wedding planning company nights and weekends, while working as a Human Resources leader for a fast-paced company during the day.

What I know now is that my body was trying to get my attention, in some ways screaming, and while no one can ever be sure, my symptoms likely showed my immune system was struggling in ways I didn't know how or make the time to support.

With hindsight, I was able to see that I'd originally gone in for a routine exam after not being seen for five years. I'm still not totally sure what made me go so long in between appointments other than I wasn't focused on family planning and had been with my husband, Chris, for 13 years at the time. He and I had started to talk about having a baby after my 30th birthday, and that was less than a year away. I'd gone in hoping to be healthy but instead learned that I was what seemed like the furthest from it, at the moment of that diagnosis call from the doctor.

My experience is that once you're told you have cancer, the world starts to feel like it's moving at a snail's crawl and lightning speed all at once. Within 30 minutes of hanging up the phone with the gynecologist, I started to get appointment calls with the oncologists she'd mentioned would be reaching out for follow-up steps. I was already spinning.

For weeks, I wept at night (and lots of days, honestly) as I shuffled in and out of appointments with different doctors, all with different opinions of what my options for treatment were. During that time, I didn't know if I was going to die, going to be fine, or anything in between. Having children was only one of many decisions and thoughts I was spinning with.

My scans ultimately showed my cancer was in an early stage, and while it was the more aggressive form, the doctor I ultimately chose was optimistic that the tumor would be removed simply, and I'd likely not need further treatment.

Most doctors recommended a hysterectomy as that was the most common treatment for cervical cancer at the time, but I was fortunate to find an oncologist who believed I was a strong candidate for a specialized surgery only done on 1300 people in the world at the time, most of them in Europe. It would preserve some of my ability to have children, and that was important to Chris and me, even if we didn't last for some reason, we didn't anticipate then but were forced to talk about. I scheduled the surgery for November 2014.

What followed in the time between was continued exams, and continued tears, until my surgery. Not really being conscious of what was happening inside me, I knew fear was gripping me tightly. I'd never had any major medical care or surgery.

Thoughts were racing through my head. What if they find more when I'm in their care? What if something goes wrong? What if I die in surgery or soon after from infection? It was all too much, too soon.

In the end, the surgery went perfectly. And after several follow-up exams, it was confirmed: no more cancer. While the fear still had its hands on me, I was able to take my first full breath since that early fall call in September.

Again, with hindsight, I see now I tried to go back to living life, almost as normally as before. I noticed myself working more than ever, but otherwise, things seemed the same. Same husband, same friends, same work, same city. But I later came to see something inside me had changed.

It would take nearly two years for me to start to see how I'd shifted from the experience, and all that I'd ultimately learn it was connected to. But once it hit my awareness, there was no way to unsee it.

Over the course of several weeks in the summer of 2016, I noticed a feeling in my body that felt like drowning. It felt like I was filled with an ocean of water from head to toe nearly every moment of every day.

After one particularly hard day, I shared how I'd been feeling with my husband; he was supportive and asked what I needed. I told him I thought I needed a weekend away. He agreed that might be good for me. I took my first solo trip ever to the San Juan Islands in Washington, not far from Portland where we lived.

After that weekend, I couldn't shake the drowning feeling. I told Chris I needed more time, this time a week. He was supportive and said he'd take care of things at home. After the week, nothing changed. I needed more time.

This time, he panicked. Chris had always seen me as consistent and stable, so this season of me being "off my footing" was new to both of us. I told him I needed a month; I knew then and even still now that in the beginning, it had nothing to do with where our relationship was. I was genuinely content and he's a great man. Any woman is lucky to have his love; I was that lucky woman for 16 years.

Ultimately Chris and I would separate and divorce, though. What I couldn't even fully see then was that through our shared cancer experience we were both thrust into about a year after his dad died from a different tumultuous cancer diagnosis, the people we'd become separately as a result, had changed. The cliche phrase "we just grew apart" still feels true.

The woman I was shifting into was initially forced by cancer's hand, but necessary for my soul. Facing my own mortality for a brief but impactful time did that, I've learned. It gave me a lot of questions, but initially not a lot of answers.

I started to ask myself things like who I was without the dream husband, house, and career. Who was I without the labels? Who was I at my core and what did I want for the future without the influence of other people's expectations or who I thought I was supposed to be for others? Who was I and what did I want for myself?

Chris and I moved in together the day after I graduated high school and ultimately married young. My high school years were spent living with a strict single dad who gave me structure and love, but not a lot of space to be a teenager and do "teenage" things. I moved in with Chris because I felt ready with him, and to escape what felt like suffocation from the expectation of always being a "good daughter."

My childhood years were often even more suffocating, growing up keeping the secret of the sexual abuse that started happening at the age of four by my grandfather. The only time I fully escaped the abuse was by spending summers with my mom after my parents divorced when I was three.

During those summers, I was also hyper-aware that she was unsuccessfully trying to hide her alcoholism. Now I know her substance use was a coping mechanism to avoid the weighty pain from her own childhood sexual abuse. During my middle school years, I thought she was healthy and told my dad that I wanted to stay with her at the end of the summer when he came to pick me up; I was hoping to have the mother/daughter relationship we'd never had before.

My dad wasn't happy with my decision but thought I was getting old enough to make some life decisions, so he agreed. But I knew standing in front of him in the driveway that hot summer day as an 11-year-old, he was doing it begrudgingly.

Very shortly after, I lost all contact with him when I learned my mom had entered a relationship with an abusive, controlling man who made sure we didn't have access to a phone and kept us moving to avoid the police due to warrants for his arrest.

In the two years before I would be reunited with my dad, there were periods of hunger, sometimes sleeping in corn fields to escape the sounds of their physical fights, police looking for me before I'd return home quietly in the morning to get ready for school without anyone knowing what was happening alongside the new experiences of sexual abuse. Years later, my mom died from her pain and the overwhelming impact alcohol had on her body.

I didn't know yet how much those experiences would come back to the surface during and after cancer. I saw a therapist in college and thought that I'd fully processed what happened in my earlier years - we'll call that belief the naivety of my youth. With my cancer experience, I could see, though, that I'd never really been able to do anything just for me. The questions that were aching inside me, THAT was the ocean-like fullness I felt in my body.

With the awareness of the ache and the reality of how precious life is now in my view, I set out on a journey to figure out who I was and who I would become as a woman. My eyes were now wide open, and there was no going back.

In the months that followed, it became clear that I needed to leave Portland, a city Chris and I moved to a few weeks after I graduated from college nearly a decade before. Portland and my life now reflected a version of me that didn't exist. We'd talked on several occasions about moving back to the Midwest after we started our family, but we knew we didn't want to go back to Detroit where we grew up.

After several months of journaling, being open to where life was taking me, and asking for guidance from the universe, part of my form of God, I had a set of serendipitous moments that pointed me toward Kansas City. I initially rejected the idea, thinking it was a coincidence and there was no way I would move to such a "podunk town" as I described it then. I was actively researching other cities: I know now that there's truth in the saying "(Wo)Man Plans, and God Laughs."

After it became abundantly clear that I needed to trust the plan bigger than me, and myself, I moved to Kansas City in the spring of 2017. I didn't know anyone when I moved. I also didn't know where life was taking me, but cancer taught me we don't control much, and there's much to be gained in surrendering to where life is taking you, and ultimately, the magic that's included in freefalling.

In the years since, I've learned that some of my family settled in Kansas and Missouri when they immigrated to the U.S. Four years in, I also remembered that the year after cancer, Chris visited Kansas for work as it's where his then company is headquartered. When he came home, he told me that we needed to visit it together because it was a really special place, and he thought I'd like it. The feeling that came over my body when he told me that would come back years later when I made the full decision to move here and again when I remembered our conversation.

Since moving to Kansas City, I've grown a tremendous amount and I believe, have stepped into becoming a woman. It didn't just happen - it's taken time, courage, intentional action, a lot of therapy in every form you can think of, pushing the edges of my comfort zone, and a lot of love from the Kansas City community - a place my heart knew I needed before my mind did.

My growth and perspective shift has fueled me personally and professionally. I've found the confidence to be my brightest self, to heal and hold any residual pain with compassion and tenderness, and to teach others to do the same. My career has shifted from being a company executive into consulting and coaching, working with companies to create human-centered workplaces, and guiding leaders to show up as their most authentic and intentional selves.

I've traveled the world, often alone, just to have the space to see things through my own eyes and be open to what my experiences are there. I've sung my lungs out at more concerts than I can count, stood on stages with thousands of people surrounding me as I shared parts of my story, made new lifelong friends, and gotten closer to my dad by learning more about each other's life experiences. I'm still best friends with Chris and hope to find another uniquely special love story like we shared again.

In the end, the call that changed my life turned out to be one of the biggest learning experiences I could've had, and I'm a better woman for it.

Jenn Toro
CEO and Founder of Spark & Sage

Jenn Toro is a visionary writer, speaker, and executive coach who specializes in fostering human-centered workplace strategies in high-growth business environments, building high-accountability cultures that become community, and driving transformative change through industrial psychology and organizational development. Guided by a deep commitment to healing and crafting a more equitable, conscious world, Jenn seamlessly integrates self-leadership with sharp business acumen to help individuals and organizations thrive.

She's been told she brings a vibrant, adventurous energy to her work, inspiring others to break free from limitations and embrace authentic, purpose-driven lives. Her passion for social impact and systemic healing is reflected in her innovative approaches, earning her recognition as a thought leader in various industry publications.

Outside of her professional endeavors, Jenn enjoys exploring new places, diving into books, and cherishing moments with her spirited 17-year-old Pug, who has been a steadfast companion through life's many highs and lows. Jenn resides near Kansas City, where she continues to inspire others to lead with purpose and compassion.

/www.linkedin.com/in/jenntoro/
www.jenntoro.com
jenn.toro@gmail.com

VICTIM BY FORCE. SURVIVOR BY CHOICE. ACTIVIST BY DESIGN

A few years ago, when we moved my mother in with our family to care for her, I was cleaning out the basement and found an old stack of papers, bound together, with a large binder clip. I leafed through the pages, reading what appeared to be journal pages of a lost soul. So much desperation spewed from each page, the ink dripping with despair. I continued to read and some of the entries seemed familiar, like I had read them before or been a witness to the emotions. As I neared the end, a startling realization hit me like a tree falling on a house. This was my journal from over twenty years prior! The person in those pages was so unfamiliar to me now, but it made me realize just how hard I had worked and how far I had come.

Perspective.

Looking back was like looking at your lawn after you finished mowing, not realizing how long the grass had grown until there was a “then” and a “now.”

I am a survivor. My abuse started as a toddler and continued for over 29 years at the hands of multiple people, people who felt my mind and body was their property to do with and coerce as they saw fit. As a result of the abuse, I endured so many legal battles and by right, became a survivor of our justice system, including criminal court, civil court, and multiple family courts.

Some people come away from trauma hardly able to function. Others pretend like nothing happened and keep it tucked away on a shelf deep in their own personal basement. Some remember every detail of what occurred while others hardly remember anything. Some become champions of a cause, and others donate what they can, but don't go too deep for self-preservation reasons. None of these are right or wrong. They just are. My path has been somewhat of a combination of most of these.

Looking back on that old journal, I clearly started out in the "hardly able to function" category. When your brain is traumatized by sexual assault at age two, things get rewired. I lived in a constant state of fear and survival, and those became my comfortable blanket of emotions. When things seemed to be going well, I would self-sabotage, so I had more trauma for which to focus. I wanted to change my behaviors and internal feelings, but fear gripped me so tightly that I didn't know how to appropriately act or react to many situations. I needed mentors.

My guides were somewhat unconventional. The movies "Desperately Seeking Susan" and "Nightmare on Elm Street" were catalysts for change and in some strange way, became subconscious mentors. Madonna's character in Desperately Seeking Susan was so wild and free. While she was certainly a hot mess, she didn't care what others thought of her and lived her life fearlessly. I wanted to live fearlessly, so in my head when I felt faced with judgment, I would ask myself, "What would Susan do?" and try to emulate some of that brazen personality.

There's a scene in "Nightmare on Elm Street" where Glen and Nancy, the two main characters besides Freddie, were on a bridge talking about the nightmares.

Nancy: *But what if they meet a monster in their dreams, then what?*
Glen: *They turn their back on it. Take away its energy and it disappears.*

It was *this* scene where I realized all of my self-sabotaging was just another form of giving my power to my abusers, even those who were no longer in my life. I had to learn how to turn my back on the internal demons and take back my power. But when you are raised in an environment where abuse is the norm, how do you even begin to learn how to find and claim your own power? For me, it was Lee Iacocca.

Lee Iacocca was the most powerful person I could think of at the time. He ran the auto industry and, without even having to say a word, commanded respect when he entered a room. I didn't want that kind of power, but I did want that level of confidence. So, whenever I was faced with a difficult situation or decision, I would mentally embody Lee, taking a deep breath, and jumping in. I mean truthfully, the biggest difference between myself and Lee (outside of age and gender) was that I was full of fear, and he had none. We both pulled our pants down to go to the bathroom and we both opened our mouths to put food in and chew. What did I really have to lose? Fear. Good riddance.

I worked in the music business for Alliance Entertainment in the New York City office in the mid-90's. I had just separated from my ex-husband and was living in a tiny apartment in downtown Spring City, Pennsylvania. I could not afford to take the train or even drive on the Turnpike, so I had to drive the four-hour (each way) commute along non-toll roads to work every day with my toddler. I used my lunch breaks to sleep, too exhausted to eat. One evening, when my daughter was with her dad, I got to stay in the city with a coworker to attend a label party. These are private events to hear one of the bands your company represents perform to an invitation-only audience. That night it was the Brand New Heavies, one of my favorite bands. Stan Miller, one of our top sales reps, knew about my long commute to and from work and was determined to introduce me to the CEO, Larry Stessel. I had way too much to drink at the party when Stan finally brought me up to Larry. He told Larry about my dedication and sacrifice and, Larry said (jokingly, I think), "Wow. Clearly, we aren't paying you enough." My inner Lee rose to the occasion, and I said, "Well, if that's how you really feel, you can put your money where your mouth is!" As soon as the words came out of my mouth, I wanted to grab them back in. What the hell just happened! Damn inner Lee.

I was deservedly and severely hung over the next morning and thought for sure I would be fired. First thing in the morning, I was called into my boss's office and gruffly told to sit down. This was it. The end of my dream job. "I don't know what you said to Larry last night, but you got a raise. Sign these papers." I was dumbfounded. Stunned. My inner Lee confidence paid off. While I don't recommend that method, it worked for me at the time. I felt a boost of confidence that would carry on to grow and flourish.

I continued to step up to embrace moments of brazen confidence and in August of 2002, I bought my first house. Leading up to that moment, took great feats of bravery.

I had been living with a guy for a year. Previously, I had lived in a fabulous old house that had been converted into six apartments. It had deep window wells that you could sit in, an enormous kitchen, and a private small porch. My best friend, Debbie, lived right down the street, and we got together with our young daughters every Wednesday night. I loved that place and my life.

In 1999, a friend and coworker introduced me to a man at a social event. He was well known in the community, a business owner, and had two young daughters, one the same age as my daughter, from a previous marriage. He was kind and loved to take me places and buy me gifts. We dated for just over a year when he asked me to move in with him. I did and that is when everything changed. His demeanor became controlling. He tried to control my money, but added that because of his business, his money would have to be separate. At the dinner table, he would pound his fist on the table to try to make his daughter eat her food. One day, he became enraged with me over something very trivial and punched the wall next to my head. Something snapped in me, and I knew I would have to get out. I started hiding cash behind photos hanging on the wall (money in plain sight but who would think to look there?). I set up a PO Box near work, I kept my passport and birth certificate in my work desk, and when I got a raise, I had the difference deposited into a new checking account I set up. I told a few people I could trust at work what was happening, as he tried to make trouble at my office a couple of times. During my lunch breaks, I would meet up with a real estate agent and go house hunting. I could not afford a large house, but I could manage to get a small one out of town so my daughter and I could be safe.

I found the perfect house and made an offer. When I closed on the house, I knew I could safely leave. That day came on August 15, 2002. He left for work, and I appeared to do the same. I turned around and went back to the house, packed up my stuff, and at lunch time, my co-workers helped me move into the house I had just bought. When he got home, he had no idea where I was. I had vanished. That was the last abusive relationship I was in.

Fast forward to 2005. Years of continued therapy and persistent hard work had been spent on my own wellbeing. I had met a wonderful man and only because I was finally happy with myself and my life without a partner, was I ready to be with him. We were married and expecting our beautiful baby girl. I continued to be bold and independent like Madonna's Susan character and work on my inner confidence like my Lee persona, while turning my back on the Freddie Krugers of the world. I worked to put my past behind me and move on with my life, not involving myself with anything having to do with domestic violence except writing an occasional check while distancing myself from trauma for self-preservation.

In 2016, a huge shift in perspective occurred. My youngest daughter built an anti-bullying app for her science fair project and won our county's elementary division, as well as the Earl S. Rommel Communications Award - she was ten years old. She called her app "Z.E.B.R.A.," an acronym for "Zoe Ending Barriers in Reporting Adversity." There was quite a bit of local press about the app and her awards. Zoho, the company's platform she used to code it, found out and invited her to speak at their Zoholics developer's conference in California in the fall of 2017. They flew our whole family out to the event.

Following the conference, Zoe was ready to go back to being a kiddo, yet I was super excited about her project's potential. That internal perspective shift was that I could no longer be passive about what happened to me but be an active participant in making things better for others. She gave me permission to use whatever I wanted minus the use of her name, so I set out to expand her concept and continue the work, shifting the focus to benefit those suffering from domestic violence and stalking. I would eventually form a company called EB*in*RA, Inc. - Ending Barriers in Reporting Adversity - as a nod to Z.E.B.R.A. while respecting her wishes.

The premise was originally supposed to be a digital diary so people could document what was happening to them and keep track of it. I am not a lawyer, but I have many friends who are. One of those friends is an employment attorney named Ayesha Hamilton. I met her for lunch one day, excited to pitch my idea and get her feedback. She listened patiently and then asked me if I had ever heard of the Daubert Standard. "No, what's that?" I asked excitedly. She explained it is the gold standard set of criteria used to determine the admissibility of expert witness testimony in federal court. According to Cornell law School:[1]

Under the Daubert Standard, the trial court considers the following factors to determine whether the expert's methodology is valid:

- *Whether the technique or theory in question can be and has been tested.*
- *Whether it has been subjected to publication and peer review.*
- *It's known or potential error rate.*
- *The existence and maintenance of standards controlling its operation; and*
- *Whether it has attracted widespread acceptance within a relevant scientific community.*

This knowledge was a huge shift for me. While researching what tools were already out there, I found many, but none that would hold up under court scrutiny to be legally admissible. This would become my new direction. I had documented so much of my life, like all those in positions of authority had directed me to do, yet none of it was allowed as evidence. It was all hearsay and the other party's attorneys had a field day with it.

I became determined to build a tool not for technology's sake, but something that could make a lasting positive impact on a victims' life. In 2018, after years of tinkering with the Z.E.B.R.A. concept, hounding endless functional experts, attending countless domestic violence-related conferences, pouring over piles of statistics and research studies, and logging huge amounts of time in business and entrepreneurial classes, I finally formed my company, EB*in*RA, Inc. While the nod to Z.E.B.R.A. was nice, it was not a memorable name. My husband used to tease me that it sounded like a pharmaceutical drug - "Ask your attorney if EB*in*RA is right for you." He thought it was funny. I had to agree. Then I met with a professional investor, and she frankly said, "No one will remember that. You need to change your name." I was pissed and slightly offended, but she was right, so I embraced my inner Sheri this time and settled for a DBA (doing business as) - VictimsVoice.

I read a report called the National Domestic Violence Prosecution Best Practices Guide (2017, rev. 2021) that said on average across the US, 80% of cases of domestic violence were dismissed, largely due to a lack of evidence. We know that most people don't report it (in 2018 it was around 77% unreported), so out of the 23% that do, only about 4-5 cases out of 100 make it to court. Most of those are offered a plea bargain for lesser charges and lesser punishment. This was the case in my own father's arrest and conviction for my 15 years of abuse and sexual assaults. He got six weekends in jail.

We have a problem with not believing victims and survivors. I was on a mission to flip that narrative and give them a legal voice when it counted the most.

When you work in technology, there's a bit of an underbelly in the startup space. Almost all the accelerator programs are focused on finding investors. I started this company before the WeWork implosion, so the pressure was high to pitch hard and break things fast. Find the big money. That didn't feel right to me, so I set out to again embrace my "Susan" and buck the system, bootstrapping the company and building it organically.

I was introduced to Charles Gattsek at a mutual friend's birthday party a year earlier, then re-introduced when I put out my intention of finding a business partner that could and would take on the role of CTO (Chief Technology Officer). Charles has his own experience with an abusive relationship so his passion for VictimsVoice was as genuine as mine. In January of 2019, he officially joined the company as my co-founder. Charles is especially talented when it comes to security and made sure all the wild-haired ideas I came up with made sense from a technical perspective and would not compromise our security or that of our users.

VictimsVoice makes all business decisions with the users' best interests at heart. We also worked hard to make sure we didn't miss anything when working through different user experiences. I am one person with my own lived experiences. At the end of the day, I am still privileged. I am Caucasian and that automatically sets me up as privileged, whether I realized it or not. This meant we had to bring a diverse group of people to the table and really listen and employ their feedback and direction. The VictimsVoice Advisory Board is composed of thirteen functional experts, including law enforcement, prosecution, finance, DEI leadership, entrepreneurial leadership, LGBTQ healthcare, nonprofit leadership, cyber security, employment law, immigration law, victim advocacy, and more. We also work(ed) with a special group of advisors, primarily Native American leaders.

VictimsVoice was always meant to serve anyone who needed it, regardless of socioeconomic status or abilities. It was built to help those being victimized collect the details of their abuse in a legally admissible way, then if the user approved it, it could help investigators collect the evidence, prosecutors build a case, and case workers and advocates understand the depth and breadth of the users' situation to ensure appropriate and lasting support.

One of the roles VictimsVoice plays is protector. Sometimes it's from abusers, sometimes it is from users, and sometimes it's for us.

The app is not really an app in the true sense. There is nothing to download so there is no icon on your phone to be discovered. As a PWA (Progressive Web App), the tool can be accessed from any device, anytime, anywhere that can connect to the internet. This lowers the barrier to entry and access. It's also a whole lot safer.

We always work under the assumption that anyone communicating with a member of our team could be the abuser pretending to be the user to gain access to the information. We protect our users from this in several ways. Number one is we never communicate with a user outside of VictimsVoice apart from this initial email verification when they first set up their account. We only communicate through an internal InMail system within the users' account which is protected by a safeword.

Sometimes our users need to be protected from themselves. When you are in an abusive relationship, there will always be a point when things blow up, then you make up and everything seems blissful. That bliss never lasts, but when it does, most people try to eliminate all documentation they may have had to not "rock the boat." The problem is the bliss always ends and then regret sets in for deleting all your evidence. We don't allow anyone to access the raw data. It stays in an encrypted state so users can rest assured, and we can prove chain of custody of the evidence.

Another way we protect our users is one of our users' biggest complaints. "Why can't I upload audio or video?!?" Not every state in the US allows recordings (audio or video) without expressed consent of all in the recording. In fact, in some states, it is a felony. We do allow for as many images as the user needs to upload to tell the story of what is happening to them and often, a picture makes for better testimony where context is concerned.

Privacy and anonymity are crucial pillars in our company. While it's easy for tech companies to collect loads of data, we only collect what is necessary to meet our mission. We also encrypt everything, so you, reading this right now, could be a user and we'd never know.

So, what do people document? Most of the time, when left to their own devices, it will be emotion-based. Why wouldn't it be, as this is a highly charged emotional situation. All the advisors with whom we collaborate make sure that the guiding questions we ask in VictimsVoice are working to collect details most people might miss. These might include questions around strangulation, animal cruelty, child endangerment, weapons (other than a knife or a gun), and more. We tie in questions to root out other potential evidence and witnesses that might have otherwise been left undiscovered.

There is always the catastrophic event where a victim does not make it. In the event this happens, we have a provision where the user can assign a designee. If assigned, the designee can request to assign a report recipient on behalf of the user to ensure their evidence is heard, even in death, medical incapacitation, or officially missing.

We have an entire portion of VictimsVoice dedicated to specific questions pertaining to Native Americans to help determine jurisdiction and legal compliance in tribal courts.

As a survivor and the CEO, it was vital that I built a tool that was victim-centric while still being able to serve those that can help victims and survivors get what they need. Too many organizations and agencies give lip service while collecting large amounts of grants and funding in the name of survivors. VictimsVoice is about serving victims directly by giving them access to a tool that puts control back into their hands. As we say in our company, "Legally admissible documentation really doesn't matter... UNTIL IT DOES."

Victim by Force. Survivor by Choice. Activist by Design.

I started moving away from my trauma, hardly able to function. I used to pretend like nothing happened, keeping it tucked away on a shelf deep inside my personal basement. I have been lucky to not remember every detail of my abuse. My brain has chosen to help me forget and I am grateful for it. But now, I do more than write the occasional check. I have created and shared VictimsVoice and championed the cause to give victims a legal voice while maintaining my own self-preservation boundaries.

I am proud of VictimsVoice. I am proud of the intentional role it plays, the lives it has changed, and the healing it has provided me and so many like me.

For more information about VictimsVoice, visit https://VictimsVoice.app

---

[1] https://www.law.cornell.edu/wex/daubert_standard#:~:text=Under%20the%20Daubert%20standard%2C%20the,%3B%20(4)the%20existence%20and

Sheri Kurdakul, SRMP

CEO, EB*in*RA, Inc. / VictimsVoice

Sheri Kurdakul, SRMP

CEO, EBinRA, Inc. / VictimsVoice

Managing Partner, Sheri Kurdakul LLC / Glitter Witch Gardens

Sheri Kurdakul is the VictimsVoice front lady, whose superpowers include taking unpopular complex problems and creating easy to use solutions that generate measurable results. She's a survivor of over 29 years of child abuse, child sexual assault, sexual assault, and domestic violence and has endured the criminal, civil, and family court system experiences.

Sheri also serves as the Managing Partner of Sheri Kurdakul LLC, an herbal company making products to empower autonomy in wellness for people, plants, and the planet.

Formerly, she was the Managing Partner of Holistic Business Solutions, a small business and nonprofit consulting firm. Sheri has spoken for many professional organizations and has published several industry papers, magazine articles, and continuing education courses.

Her focus now is on making a measurable difference in the lives of victims and survivors so their abusers can be held accountable, and they can begin to reclaim and rebuild their lives in safety and on their own terms.

https://www.linkedin.com/in/sherikurdakul/
https://www.instagram.com/victimsvoiceapp/
SheriK@EBinRA.com
https://VictimsVoice.app

HOW TO TAKE CONTROL OF YOUR LIFE STORY

There are two main ideas that I always try to portray to the patients that I work with. First, stories do not exist in isolation. They are interwoven amongst our experiences, our relationships, our emotions and thoughts, our family dynamics, our hopes, our fears. These stories are the driving forces of our lives. Often, these stories are problem-saturated narratives that focus on the person as the center of the problem. This brings me to my second idea I want my patients to know: we are never the problem; the problem is always the problem. In a world in which we are taught to internalize aspects of who we are, it becomes very easy for us to become the problem at the center of our life story. It took many, many years for me to take these two concepts and believe them at the core of who I am. It is still a struggle on some days, but I make it a daily practice to remind myself.

When I was asked to write a chapter for Agents of Social Change, I thought it would be easy. I have spent my entire professional career writing hundreds of pages in published research, essays for my doctoral program, psychological report write-ups, and everything in between. What I did not anticipate was the amount of emotions that it would bring up for me. I felt it was important to write about my own experiences and how they shaped me into the psychologist that I am today before providing some ways in which you can be an agent of social change in your own life. There is often an air of ego amongst the mental health field that prohibits clinicians from sharing their personal life experiences. I have always been nothing but transparent about my own journey and path in hopes that it will help someone else. It is important that I never ask any patient to do anything that I have not done or would not be willing to do.

My identity consists of many things. I am a clinical psychologist. I am a gay man. I am a recovering alcoholic. Among the many parts of my identity, these three have completely shattered the course of my life and turned it upside down. Although it took many years and reflection to understand why this was necessary (hindsight is 20/20!), I am finally in a space where I can sit back and connect the dots without wanting to change anything. The path of me becoming an agent of social change required these growing pains.

Growing up as a gay man in the conservative, midwestern state of St. Louis was not an easy thing. One of my very first memories around the age of four or five was that I felt a gravitational pull, for lack of a better description, towards males in a photo. In that exact same memory, I remember feeling like what I felt and what I was pulled to was inherently wrong. I remember making a conviction at that young age to never tell a soul about this part of me. At that point in time, I made myself the problem. It is interesting to reflect on. My parents never shamed the queer community, and I never saw anything shameful about the queer community in the media in my early years. Maybe it was the lack of representation in the world around me, or maybe it was just how it was to grow up as a gay man in that area. As I said in the beginning, these stories do not exist in isolation.

I remember being in 2nd grade and someone asked me if I was gay. I didn't even know what that word meant yet, but I knew by the tone of their voice that they seemed to discover my deepest secret. My stomach dropped. My heart started racing. I wanted to cry. I uttered back a quick, "I don't know what you are talking about," and then I ran away and avoided them for the rest of the school year. I thought that I could avoid anyone who seemed to point out my higher-pitched voice or my lack of interest in typical male things. Eventually, I ran out of places to run. I thought that if I avoided the question enough, people would stop bullying me and treating me like I was a problem. I was wrong.

I remember being in 5th grade and realizing that all my friends were girls. I was supposed to have a party that year for my birthday and I was paralyzed by the idea that only girls would be there. Again, I was never taught that having all female friends was bad; I just had a belief that this would somehow lead to my secret being discovered, or that this was somehow not "normal" or "right." At that same party in 5th grade, I set a tradition. I would wish to be straight for every birthday candle blowout. I thought that maybe after enough birthdays this would come true. I was wrong.

I remember entering 6th grade and I had my mom throw out my entire closet. I went to Abercrombie & Fitch and bought 6 colored polos and a few pairs of ripped jeans. My sister's friend had been dressing in this look all summer, and I wanted to do my best to imitate what I thought other straight men would wear. I wore those same few outfits for a year. Maybe this would protect me from people yelling slurs about me being a "fa**t," or someone that no one wanted around. I was wrong.

I remember going to a party in 7th grade with a bunch of my "popular" female friends. As always, I felt like the tag-along person that nobody else outside wanted there outside of my few friends. I showed up at that party not knowing a single person besides the four people I came with. Within about ten seconds, I was told by a friend that I had 30 seconds to leave the party before I got beat up. When I asked why, my friend told me, "He thinks you are gay, and he cannot stand gay people." I tried to say that I was not gay, and I didn't even know him. It did not matter, I had to leave. I walked out to the driveway alone, too ashamed to call my family for help and too paralyzed by the fear of getting physically hurt. My "friends" had told me they wanted to stay at the party and did not know how I could get home, but that I had to figure it out. 30 seconds later, I got a text that said, "Run." as I stood in the driveway of someone's house who I did not know. Without thinking, I sprinted for 30 minutes across the highway.

Alone. In an area I did not know. To this day, I am not sure why I was told to run and what would have happened if I didn't. In my mind, I would have been beaten to a pulp just for existing. I ended up walking around for six hours by myself along the highway in 7th grade thinking of all of the ways that I was the problem. Ironically, I ended up apologizing to my "friends" for making them have to deal with me. I thought maybe someone would finally stand up for me. I was wrong.

I remember the first time that I was beaten up. It was at a party in my freshman year of high school. Someone that I did not know walked up to me and told me he needed to talk to me in the parking lot. I sensed that something was wrong, so I said, "No, I am okay. Thanks." As I turned around, I felt a massive swing to my jaw that dropped me to the ground. At the point in time, I would try harder and harder to be a wallflower to not have to endure the embarrassment of being punched in the face in front of fifty people without a single person coming to my defense. Maybe if I just shrunk myself enough, people would see that I just want to fit in and I hate this part of me, too. I was wrong.

In addition to my experiences of being a gay man, I also have a very distinct memory of the first time that I used alcohol to escape the inner shame of my sexuality. I was fourteen years old, and it was a hot summer day. My friend had brought over a bottle of vodka. I had had a few sips of alcohol prior to this, but never anything that led to a mind-altering experience. I immediately downed half the bottle of vodka. I am not sure what called me to drink so much in so little time. Maybe it was that I knew it would help me escape. Maybe it was just stupidity. All I remember is that for those 2 hours before my memory escaped me, it was the first time in my life that I did not worry about how others perceived me.

My family used to joke and tell me that my "inner sassy person" came out when I drank. It really did. For someone who spent every moment from their earliest memories to that first time blacking out obsessing over hiding this secret and being careful of how others portrayed me, it was like a million pounds was lifted off of my shoulders. I needed that weightless experience again. Again. Again. And again.

Little did I know that this would kick start the next 8 years of substance abuse. I would spend every waking moment going forward thinking about how I could “check out.” Sometimes it was marijuana, sometimes it was pills, sometimes it was alcohol. It didn’t matter what it was as long as it helped me to not think about what I was going through. When I turned 18 and finally came out to my parents (which was extremely well received ☺), I had already started down the path to addiction and there was no turning around. I was arrested multiple times for underage possession of alcohol, stealing alcohol from Walmart, possession of marijuana, and many other petty charges. I spent many, many nights in jail only to be bailed out the next day by parents who wanted to hope that I would finally learn my lesson. Eventually, it all caught up to me. When I was eighteen, I was arrested for the final time related to drugs. I was in denial of the seriousness of my charges. I thought that I could use my previous ability to talk and pay my way out of problems again. Not this time. I was put on probation and would spend the next 3 years showing up to my probation officer drunk, manipulating my way out of situations, and doing everything that I could to avoid the problem. Eventually, I reached a point where I knew that I would have to spend time in jail for messing up my probation. Being more afraid to go to jail than I was to die from my drinking, I made a decision to go to treatment. Once I texted my family and told them I was an alcoholic who needed help, there was no going back. I wanted to take my power back.

Now, the point of all of this is not to try and obtain pity or sympathy for experiences that I went through. I have integrated these experiences into my life so that they are just moments that have foraged my path forward. My truth is that I would not change my earlier experiences of shame and guilt and disgust towards myself for anything. I would not change the countless experiences of blacking out just so I would not feel the suffering anymore. If I want to talk about being an agent of social change, it is important to talk about the moments in my life that called me into being this agent. I have to talk about the moments that led me to taking my power back. The power that I gave away to anyone who told me that I was not loveable because I was gay. The power that I gave away to alcohol, thinking that it would take away my pain without destroying my life in the process. The power that I gave away so freely to anyone who validated my own internal suffering and shame.

It is all an illusion anyways, isn't it? The idea that other people can actually have our power and our worth. What I needed to realize through this process was that these things are internal. They have always been internal. No one can actually take away our own power and our own worth. We simply deceive ourselves into thinking that this is the case. Reaching a point of desperation that called for the reclaiming of my power and my worth was the moment I started being an agent of social change.

A lot has happened in my life since I came out as a gay man and admitted to being an alcoholic. I am in a loving partnership. I have eight years of continuous sobriety. I am a Doctor of Clinical Psychology and work as part of a team and in my own private practice. Much of my daily lived experience is in the realm of helping other people become their own social agents of change. Although I initially began writing about my earlier experiences that thrusted me into being an agent of change, I have realized that my driving force in life has been a calling to help other people realize their own power for change. It is to help people realize that they *can* have control over their own agency in life.

My patients often ask me how they can have a better life, when what they really seem to want is an easier life. Everyone seems to ask for little tricks and hacks for how life can feel easier, mistakenly thinking that this also makes it better. And I get it. I really do. I sometimes just want an easier life, too. The irony, however, is that the life that people often come to me desperately seeking to find is not found in these fast-tracked ways of healing and "top 5 tricks to cure depression" blog posts that they frantically search. It is not found in the quick fixes and self-help books that serve as distractions from doing the actual hard work. It is found in the day in and day out work and tenacity of the process. It is found in the discipline and practice of necessary things on a daily basis that help you to live life to the fullest. Often, these are not things that we want to do. And I get it. I do not usually want to do them as well.

A better life is found in the ability to tolerate and sit with discomfort instead of trying to avoid it. It is found in figuring out how to set boundaries instead of escaping them. It is diving into uncomfortable stuff and breaking patterns instead of keeping the status quo. It is holding space for the emotionally charged situations instead of seeking out the external to pacify yourself. And none of this is easy. Start to pay attention. When you want something to be better, do you look for the easier way or the better way?

So, how do we work on becoming an agent of social change? What tips could I pass on as a psychologist that helps to teach people how to become an agent of change in their own life? Here are a few places to start. These do not serve as a "get out of therapy and hard work" card, but rather as places to start thinking and exploring.

Externalization of the problem is key. This is the process of separating yourself from the problem. It is hard to be an agent of social change when you are constantly thinking that you are the problem. How do we escape a problem that we feel is inherent to who we are, that we feel is embedded in our bones and DNA? When people tell me that they want to take charge of their life but the [insert problem] is taking control, I tell them to separate themselves from it. You are not the problem. Depression is the problem. The anxiety is the problem. The addiction is the problem. Using this language, by calling and naming it in a way that feels comfortable for you, allows you to take a different perspective on your identity and how the problem is impacting you. I have some patients call their problems by human names (e.g., Fred). I have others describe it as things (e.g., the black hole). Instead of saying, "I am depressed," try saying, "the depression is really strong right now." Over time, this separation from the problem helps to distance you from feeling like you are the issue at hand. Remember, we are never the problem. The problem is the problem.

Always stay curious. I preach to my patients that curiosity is the answer to so many problems. So often we look through things from a lens of shame or some sort of negatively skewed perception. Approaching things from curiosity helps us to take agency over our lives and break negative feedback loops and patterns. For instance, instead of being upset and shameful at how you acted in a situation, try being curious about why you were upset and shameful about how you acted. What was the most upsetting part? What does this say about what is important to you? How can you remain curious so that you can view your life through a lens that actually serves your process in being your own social agent of change?

Find unique outcomes. Essentially, this means that you look for times in your life when a problem has less of a grip on you than other times. I always operate from a lens that no problem has 100% control over your life. What are the times in which the problem is 10% less? Are there any times in which the problem is nonexistent? What is it about these times that allow for this? Naturally, patients will tell me that these times do not exist. If you cannot find any unique outcomes in your life, what would it *look and feel like* to find these times?

Think about your preferences. It always amazes me that when I ask questions of preference, people usually struggle to identify them. How can we start creating change in our life if we are not able to identify what we want that life to even look like? Questions of preference simply means that you start to decide what you want things to look like. What is your preference for how your marriage would be? What is your preference for your relationship to your mental health? What is your preference for how you view intimacy? Once you identify these preferences, you can start to look at what is standing in the way of these preferences. We cannot move to a new path without first outlining that path.

Although this is a brief and non-exhaustive list of areas to explore to start being the agent of change in your own life, it can be a helpful place to start. We are all the writers of our own stories, and so often these stories are problem-saturated and negatively skewed. Because the human experience does not exist without stories, we tell ourselves, we have to start paying attention to what these stories are. Examining how these stories came to be and seeking to build self-serving, self-preferred stories can have a massive impact on creating waves in your own life.

So, why does this all matter? It matters because the life stories we curate are the driving force of our lives. Because so many people are unaware of what their narratives are. These stories don't exist in isolation. They are intertwined and often filled with problem-saturated narratives. It matters because many of these life narratives focus on the person as the center of the problem. People are not the problem; the problem is the problem. If you don't believe in the deepest parts of your heart that you are not the problem, and that your struggles are just a result of social and personal interactions and experiences, then the change you want to see won't come to fruition.

What now? The work lies in exploring human possibilities rather than settled certainties. Every time we ask a question, we are generating a possible version of life. Remain curious. Work to find outcomes in which the problem is lessened in influence and use these to build a story in which you are capable, in control, and able to handle and lead your preferred way of living.

And lastly, it is important to know that *you make complete sense*. I always instill this into everyone that I meet. What you are feeling makes sense. The problems you are dealing with make sense. The hopes and preferences you have make sense. Take back your power and worth and start designing your preferred life. I believe in you. You got this.

DR. TONY MEINERS Psy.D.

Dr. Tony Meiners is a licensed clinical psychologist who has spent the last decade of his career working in residential, PHP, IOP, and outpatient levels of care. He brings a holistic treatment methodology to his treatment with patients to promote an integrative approach. He has a private practice in Newport Beach, CA and serves as the Clinical Director of a residential treatment program specializing in the treatment of trauma and stress-related disorders. Dr. Meiners utilizes his queer and neurodivergent-specific training in conjunction with knowledge of neurobiological and cognitive treatment modalities to help heal clients.

On his philosophy of his approach as psychologist, he states, "I am a firm believer in the idea that we are all the authors of our own story and have the power to change the narratives that are no longer serving our best interests. I strive for a collaborative environment with the individuals I work with and believe that they are the experts in their own lives. So often, individuals make themselves the center of the problem. Our problems don't define us; we define our problems. It is the process of separating themselves from the problem and discovering alternative stories to their lives that allows individuals to step into their most desired state of being. My hope is that my clients can create a more self-serving narrative that encompasses their strongest preferences for the life they want to lead, one full of new meanings and rich possibilities."

UNIVERSITIES + DEGREES: [Doctor of Applied Clinical Psychology, Psy.D.] The Chicago School of Professional Psychology. [Master of Social Work, Adult Mental Health and Wellness Concentration] University of Southern California. [Bachelor of Psychology] Maryville University.

CLINICAL SPECIALIZATION: His areas of specialty include bottom-up and top-down conjunctive treatment by combining somatic and/or experiential based interventions with post-modern cognitive therapeutic modalities. His work centers around identity development for individuals that exist in constructs outside societal expectations. In addition, queer-affirming and neurodivergent-affirming approaches to the treatment of trauma are his current areas of focus and treatment.

TRAININGS: Trauma Resiliency Model; Eye Movement Desensitization and Reprocessing; Narrative Therapy; Holographic Reprocessing; Safe and Sound Protocol

drtonymeiners@gmail.com
drtonymeiners.com
@drtonymeiners
Publications: Dissertation: *Relationship Between HIV Status and Substance Use Recovery Among Gay Men*

THERE'S NO PLACE LIKE HOME

Living in Black and White

How many times have you watched the Wizard of Oz? Do you even know? I don't. I just know that every year around Thanksgiving time it was on TV, and I NEVER missed it. A younger Amy loved the magical ruby slippers, the sparkle of Glenda's pink tulle gown, and even the scary flying monkeys. But go back and watch it as an adult and you will see a whole different story. One of overcoming adversity, facing your fears, and finding out what really matters. I found myself thinking of Dorothy as I was facing my own adversity and fears and taking stock of my self-worth as I went through one of the hardest times in my life...a divorce, So, I decided to go on my own journey down the yellow brick road. Maybe to see what was on the other side, but more importantly to see what was inside...me.

You may remember that the movie starts off in black and in white. The gray tones and shadows are deliberate to set the tone of a life for Dorothy that to state the obvious, lacked color. And so, I found myself in the same boat as Dorothy in the last few years of my life. Living in black and white. Don't get me wrong, my ex-husband was and is a good man. I wasn't abused or cheated on. To onlookers, we were a charismatic, beautiful, and successful couple. It is true that no one really knows the insides of a marriage except the two people in it. And to be honest, I'm not even sure we knew or were willing to admit the troubles that lurked like flying monkeys in the darkness of the forest.

The reality was we had issues for years. Countless hours of marriage therapy, couple's bible studies, intensive marriage retreats, and even our own attempts to "reignite" our relationship with date nights and vacations. But none of it sustained. For the last 3 years, we were great friends and partners. In fact, we were roommates. I craved affection and intimacy. He craved acceptance. It just wasn't working. And so, one day after weeks of self-exploration and talking with a life coach, I decided to leave my husband. I was finally starting to see what my life could be like. How I could BE. How I could feel. It was like the moment that Dorothy opened the door after the house landed in Munchkinland. It was like my mind and heart were opened and I saw the possibility of a life in full color.

In the movie, the tornado takes Dorothy to Munchkinland. But in my story, it was a bit out of sequence. I started to see life in full color and then the tornado hit like a freight train. The tornado of the separation and ultimately the decision he made to divorce. All I can say is it felt like everything a tornado is; destructive, unpredictable, fucking scary as hell and makes you wonder if you will live or die.

The Twister

In The Wizard of Oz, right before the tornado hits, Dorothy says to Toto, "Let's go someplace where there isn't any trouble." Well, Dear Dorothy, your trouble was just starting. As soon as I told my husband I wanted to separate, it was like the biggest storm and deadly tornado hit. My husband was angry and hurt (understandably), some people even stopped talking to me and of course everyone was feeling sorry for him and villainizing me.

I packed some bags and moved to a friend's house while my husband and I decided to enlist a marriage counselor to help us to discern if we should stay together. Honestly, that first week is a blur. I barely ate or slept, and my stomach felt like it was constantly eating me alive from the inside out. I lost 20 pounds in a matter of a month as my body succumbed to the anxiety and pure anguish. My life felt like it was completely out of control. I spent 3 weeks in a spiral of hope, despair, hope, despair, hope, despair. Round and round and round like a tornado. It was one of the lowest times of my life.

My girlfriend was coming back from Canada, so it was time for me to leave her place and move on. My apartment wouldn't be ready for move-in for 6 weeks, so I decided to take a road trip to try to create some geographic distance from what was happening and to be intentional about healing. And the other thing I wanted to be intentional about...learning to let go of control. Here I was no marriage, no job and no place to live. I felt like everything was stripped away from me. It was clear the universe/God was holding up a big neon sign saying to me, "Girl, you have got to learn to surrender." And so, I did just that.

Down on the Farm

I packed up my car and headed out on my Yellow Brick Road Trip on a sunny Georgia Saturday morning. You might be thinking, "oh how exciting to be going on a road trip", but to be honest, I felt a bit uneasy. I was intentional that this would be a trip where I would dig in and look at the ugly, scared, wounded me. So, to say that I was excited would just not be true. It was going to be hard. It was going to be really hard. I had done some research on the best podcasts on divorce and life after divorce and had bookmarked a number of episodes. So, as I pulled out of the driveway, I reluctantly started the first podcast.

As I passed milepost after milepost and listened to podcast after podcast on divorce, I found myself listening to a podcast that featured Peter Crone, the mindset life coach. I had never heard of him before but as I listened to his words, I was reminded of the last 2 years of spiritual growth I had experienced by reading and listening to Eckhart Tolle. Peter's words washed over me and there was a resonance that I felt, almost a coming back to soul. I spent the next 5 hours driving and listening to every podcast I could find that featured Peter Crone. And with each passing mile I felt the sadness and despair start to lift.

By the time I got to the Women's Retreat Art Farm outside Paducah I could feel the shift. I parked next to my cute little red cottage where I would stay for the night and looked out over the fields. The peace that settled in my soul was palpable. I unloaded and then took a walk on the farm. There was a lovely breeze, and the sun was shining among big fluffy clouds. I stepped into the field and just soaked in the sun and the feeling of being lighter. I could feel the shift. I could feel the healing of my heart, as strange as it sounds. I was starting to see things with new eyes. Not just things... myself, my current situation, my soon to be ex and my future. And it was freeing.

Peter Crone says, "What happened, happened and couldn't have happened any other way.... because it didn't." In essence things are as they are so what good does it do to lament what happened or what is happening, it just creates more suffering. Eckhart Tolle says, "What you resist, persists." It's the same concept. I was lamenting and resisting what had happened and what was happening, and I was doing nothing but creating more suffering for myself. I had a choice on how to view my circumstances.

Another quote that hit me during the Peter Crone podcasts was, "Life will present you with people and circumstances to reveal where you're not free." And Eckhart has said, "Whatever the current moment, accept it as if you had chosen it yourself." So, I had a choice. I could choose to look at my life circumstances as a victim or I could view it as a gift to see where I am stuck in my patterns and grow into more of the person, I am at my soul level. I stood in that field and started to make that choice. And it felt right.

Lions and Tigers and Bears! Oh My!

For over 3 months I lived in a prison of my mind. A prison of fear. It was like when Dorothy and her friends enter the dark forest and the Scarecrow says, "Of course, I don't know, but I think it will get darker before it gets lighter." And boy, did it!

I was spiraling in fear of, "Where will I live? I don't have a job, I'm being abandoned, I don't have any money." The underlying thought and fear were lurking below the surface...I am not enough; I am not loveable. I would spiral in the depths of these thoughts and feel helpless and hopeless. Consumed. And I bought into those thoughts repeatedly.

Just like Dorothy I am blessed with a circle of friends who held me up, loved me and gave me courage to get through the next moment, the next hour, the next day. She had the Scarecrow, The Lion and the Tin Man...and of course, Toto. I had 6 or 7 women and even some of their husbands who listened to me, cried with me, counseled me, fed me, gave me a place to sleep and in general just loved on me. Each of my friends brought their own gifts in each interaction with me. One friend called me every day to check on me. Another friend let me stay at her house while she was away. Another friend acted as my life coach. Another friend gave me pep talks and built my confidence while another friend provided a presence of calm and serenity for me to feel safe. And other friends showed up BIG for me by providing divorce law and tax and financial planning advice. For 3 months my web of support tended to my broken heart and slowly helped me pick up the pieces and put myself back together. It's like the Japanese art of Kintsugi where pottery that is broken is put back together using gold and is considered even more beautiful than before. My friends were there by my side helping me pick up the broken pieces and putting the gold joinery in my cracks. There was a new piece of art forming. And like Dorothy, it was always inside me, I just had to be broken to discover it.

The Lure of Poppy Fields

There is a scene in The Wizard of Oz where the Wicked Witch of the West creates a poppy field to try to keep Dorothy and her troupe from reaching the Emerald City. The group starts through the field commenting on the beauty all around them. Little do they know the colorful and seemingly innocent flowers are laced with toxins that will put you to sleep. Each of the friends slowly falls into a deep slumber.

Is life really that different? We all go through our lives looking for ways to distract ourselves from our pain or stay asleep. We drink, overeat or don't eat at all, we work 12 hours a day, we binge on Netflix, and the most common distraction technique...we make ourselves BUSY. Why? Because doing those things is easier and a lot less scary than actually having to feel our feelings or face our fears.

As I have been on this Yellow Brick Road Trip, I have had an opportunity to look at where I was asleep and where I was in fight or flight in my own life. I am able to see now that I was living in my story of my childhood fears and using that filter in all of my relationships. (Spoiler alert: We all do this!) It's like we are looking at our lives through a specific shade of glasses, a shade of our story we have created. So, my story was, people will abandon me, people won't love me, I am unlovable. (Another spoiler alert: almost all of us have the same core filter of "I'm not loveable, I'm not good enough.") However, it shows up differently for each of us. For me, I used to judge others because I was really judging myself. For my husband it was not being vulnerable to people because they would eventually hurt him. For others it may be manipulation or withdrawal or aggression or addiction.

I decided to dig in on my own NGE (Not Good Enough) behavior and I was blown away. I saw my underlying judgment and criticism of others and my confrontational behavior and it made me so sad. I used that behavior because I felt unsafe and thought if I did those things it would keep me from being abandoned. Here's the kicker...it then becomes a self-fulfilling prophecy. Hear this! The hurt you are trying to avoid you are actually creating through your actions. When I would judge others, they would pull away, understandably and I would then feel abandoned, the one feeling I was trying to avoid at all costs. Well, fuck!

But here is the good news. Awareness is the key. And just like when Glenda the Good Witch sent rain to wash away the toxic scent of the poppies, awareness is washing away my self-made-up story. The story I had created of the little girl who was abandoned and needed to control her life and others to not get hurt. I immediately started to take accountability for my actions with the people I love. I wrote my husband (about to be ex-husband) a letter of accountability and apology for how I showed up and the pain it caused him. I also had a healing conversation with my mother about a difficult time in our relationship. Those conversations were a turning point for me to reframe my story, start taking accountability and stop being the victim. AND IT WAS BOTH HEALING AND FREEING. Part of this process was to also have compassion for myself for my actions of the past. The reality is that I was acting at the level of my awareness. We all are. So how can I criticize myself or others for acting from their own pain and level of awareness. We are all doing the best we can at the time. Jesus said, "Forgive them Lord, for they know not what they do." And that is the truth. Have compassion for yourself and others because we are all just doing the best we can at the time.

I wish awareness was the cure. It is the diagnosis and a huge part in the healing and starting to live your life from a place of love instead of fear. But the real work comes in identifying the patterns when they start to sprout up...and they will. I have 53 years of programming those patterns. I have carefully and ardently created them and reinforced them with outside circumstances and people. So, it is only natural that they will pop up. And so, I have been like a scout on a safari searching for animals. I'm looking for tracks, smelling for the scent, analyzing the dung or scat on the trail. Meaning, anytime I start to feel scared, anxious, angry or worried, I stop. I sit with the emotion and ask, "What am I feeling?" Ok, now let's look at why I am feeling that way. Thirdly, what from my old story is creating or supporting those thoughts and feelings? And last, are they really true? And the answer is NO. It is always NO. And then I use my tools that I have found that bring me back to the center of the real truth...I am enough. I am loveable.

Back on the Yellow Brick Road

One of my stops on my road trip was in a tiny town in Indiana where I planned to camp at an Alpaca Farm. The farm is owned by a single woman who is a retired vet. She was an officer and served in Iraq. Her name is Tracy.

I pulled into Aris Farm and I saw Tracy at the end of a paddock. She walked over to greet me followed by a string of dogs and cats. There was a great Pyrenees, a beagle, an orange-colored mutt, a little chihuahua, an orange kitten and a big orange cat with pale green eyes surrounding Tracy. We exchanged greetings and she took me on a tour of the farm.

The property has these massive oak trees that must be over 200 years old which frame the barn area. As we walked around the farm Tracy told me about the personalities of each of the 25 alpacas, the llamas, the 2 pigs, the miniature horses and donkeys and called each of the 15 goats by name. The alpacas are curious creatures and very docile. I couldn't get over how the tuft of hair on the top of their heads made them look like a guy from a 60's band. One in particular, named PJ gave me multiple kisses. I fell in love. Animals know how to heal. They just do. And I let myself be covered in the healing from each beautiful animal soul I encountered that evening. It was magical. By the time Tracy had finished the tour, we had both shared our life stories and were standing in the goat paddock crying. It was a moment of beautiful connection that I will treasure forever.

Family and Farmland

There is something about the farmland of the Midwest...and the people. After leaving the alpaca farm in Indiana I headed to the tiny college town of Gambier, Ohio where my aunt and uncle live on 10 acres in the middle of a variety of crops. My Aunt is a retired art professor from Kenyon College and even at 78 she is still a very successful artist. Her art studio is located on the second story of a renovated barn in front of their beautiful home.

I intentionally chose to visit my Aunt and Uncle because I knew they would provide a safe and healing space for me. My Aunt and I have grown increasingly close over the past 2 years while engaging in conversations and a book club on "A New Earth", by Eckhart Tolle. I have always had such a fondness for my aunt, but this brought our relationship to new depths. She was also so loving and supportive in the weeks and months during my marriage separation and when my husband told me he wanted to divorce. I would call her sobbing, and she would just listen and give me space to be sad. Then she would calmly give me words of love and support.

You've Had the Power All Along, My Dear

I had a lot of time to think while on the road trip. Whether it was behind a windshield, walking through crops, or just sitting looking at nature. Thoughts can be nasty little creatures if you let them grab hold of you. They can take you down a spiral in as little as 10 seconds. And I had plenty of spirals.

In this way, I have been a lot like Dorothy. I knew I had the power to change my thoughts, but I just couldn't access it. I had to go through the journey and the suffering to fully realize and actualize it. Let's be honest, it is not easy to be handed a bag of lemons and be able to quickly and easily change your thoughts to envision tasty lemonade. But it can be done. It is a choice. And yes, I have to make the choice over and over again.

While at my aunt's house, I had a bit of an epiphany. When something ends in our life, we tend to look at it as a loss. In reality, is it a loss or is it just an ending? For example, did you lose a loved one or did they die? If you believe that their soul lives on then they have not been lost, they are just in a different form. Your grief and suffering will be much more severe with the first thought vs the second thought. So, did I really lose my husband and my marriage, or did it just end? I thought about this, and it dawned on me that I really lost my marriage 2 years before. We had essentially been roommates and friends for the last 2 years, so I didn't actually lose anything recently. In fact, we are still friends, we are just not going to be married and be roommates anymore. Being in my marriage there was a lot of pain for me wanting to have an intimate relationship and being faced every day with not being able to have it. Realizing I don't have to experience that anymore brought a wash of relief over me.

This choice of how to think about my marriage and divorce brought such a sense of relief and peace. I had the power to think this way all along, but sometimes, just like Dorothy, you have to go through the dark forest to come out into the light. I also knew this wouldn't be the last time

I would have to make a choice about how I think and feel about the end of my marriage, but at least I knew I had the power inside me. In fact, it had been there all along, my dear.

There's No Place Like Home

After a month of traveling from Atlanta to Paducah to Kansas City, Indiana to Ohio to Alabama and North Carolina, it was finally time to return home. Home. What a loaded, complex, layered word. I was going back to stay at the house with my future "wasband" for a few days until he left for a business trip. We had agreed I would stay at the house to watch the dogs while he was away. I also had to start packing for my move in one week.

As I was driving back from North Carolina I could feel the creeping dread and anxiety of the negative thoughts rising up, "I have to go back to this house. I have to be around him while I am so sad. I have to start packing to permanently leave a home that I lovingly curated. And I have no job and no idea of what my life will look like." I had spent the previous 3 weeks interviewing for a job at my ideal company, among others. Four grueling rounds of interviews culminated with a panel presentation the day before. Although I thought I did ok in the presentation, I just didn't think I had done enough to land the job. More defeating thoughts. Ten minutes before I pulled into the driveway of the house, I got a call from my ideal company offering me the job. Now THAT is God! The Universe knew I needed something to look forward to. I was glowing with excitement, relief, and anticipation. I was hopeful.

Was I elated? Yes! But here is where the real story comes in. Yes, I was so thankful that God/The Universe had shown me grace. But the last few months and particularly the last month had taught me the most important lesson of all. I know now that there is no job, no house, and no one that can make me feel ok. There is nothing external that can make you ok or even not ok because all those things are transient. Houses come and go, jobs come and go, and even relationships come and go. The only thing that makes you ok is YOU. And THAT is HOME. Once you realize that, you see that is the power. That is where real peace lies and there is no place like home. YOU ARE HOME. You always have been.

Dorothy Goes to the Jungle

As I mentioned, while on my road trip I was very intentional about listening to signs from God/Universe and also tapping more into my intuition. That word "intuition" is thrown around a lot but being able to actually be quiet and still enough to know what is right and true versus fear is something we all have, we just have to tune it like an instrument to let it play the song that sits inside us.

As I was listening to podcasts, reading books, listening to music and talking with friends, the topic of ayahuasca as a healing medicine kept coming up. I had a few friends that had told me over the years about their own healing experiences with ayahuasca. I had always had these visions of them in a teepee with shamans and smoke billowing out of the tent flap. Of course, that is not at all how an ayahuasca retreat looks...at least not the one I attended. As I kept hearing about it, I just knew in my soul that this was the next and probably biggest step in my healing journey.

At the recommendation of a trusted friend, I applied (yes, applied) to attend a retreat in Costa Rica where Ayahuasca is legal. You have to apply because this particular retreat wants participants who will be intentional about their healing and what they take back into the world.

This retreat is attended by executives, professionals, entrepreneurs, doctors and other people in the medical field. These are not drug addicts or hippies. They are people who understand that plant medicine has been used for centuries and can be an effective alternative to big pharma pills and treatments. All you have to do is Google psychedelics and healing, and you will find all kinds of research on the effectiveness of these types of medicines on PTSD, depression, anxiety, OCD and more.

I had no idea of what to expect and I was nervous, to say the least. But I was also sure that I wanted to heal my core wounds and rewire my brain to live a free life. Spoiler alert: I healed more in one week at this retreat than I did in 20 years of therapy. That is how impactful this medicine is. I could write a whole book on my week-long journey with "Grandmother Ayahuasca", as the medicine team calls her. They call her that because she is ancient and also loving. But I am here to let you know that it is a safe and effective option for healing. There are other healing modalities that are also effective, such as therapy, breathwork, meditation, ketamine, etc. But this is the one that is generally viewed as the most effective and transformative in a short period of time.

I want people to know that plant medicine, like any drug, if used responsibly can be more effective at healing all kinds of diseases and especially dis-ease of the mind and heart. We all have things from our past that have left an imprint on our minds and affect how we see circumstances and people now. The medicine helps you become aware of those wounds and rewires the brain to integrate those wounds into a healthier and more fulfilled holistic you.

That is what I have experienced. My time with Grandmother Aya has been a beautiful journey of coming home to myself. I started the road trip with an awareness of my core wounds which led me to acceptance and understanding. But it was ayahuasca that had helped to re-wire those pathways in my brain of not feeling good enough. It was the medicine that took me past all the filters that I have built over 54 years and let me see the perfect, loveable, beautiful me. My experience with ayahuasca has helped me see that I have been there all along and just like Dorothy, I just had to look inside.

CEO of nothing. Student of everything. Also a Transformation Coach and Certified Conscious Leadership Consultant

Amy IG is a seasoned life and business coach with 30 years of impactful experience, having positively influenced over 50,000 lives across 35 countries. Recognized internationally for her coaching and training excellence, Amy founded Unlocking Venus to create supportive circles for women transitioning from worry to wonder. She also offers personalized 1:1 coaching for those seeking growth in their personal or professional lives. Additionally, Amy conducts conscious leadership workshops for corporations to impact culture and productivity. Outside of her professional endeavors, she finds joy in nature, animals, and a good queso dip.

Amy Impara-Gregory
www.amyimparagregory.com
www.unlockingvenus.com
aiconsulting@yahoo.com
https://www.facebook.com/unlockingvenus
https://www.instagram.com/amyigjustlove/

FROM PAIN TO PURPOSE, THE STORY OF GIVING HOPE & HELP

Greetings! Thank you for taking a bit of your time to visit my chapter.
My life experiences with my heavy cycle, fibroids, sexual assault as a teen, that I hid for 20 years, domestic violence as a young adult, and losing my dear friend to domestic violence, empowered me to turn my pain into purpose. These experiences resulted in my assignment to speak and take action, so that I could make a difference in the world. I knew one of my assignments was to speak for the voiceless including, giving sound to my own voice that had not spoken. My assignments including transposing pain from my experiences into purpose to make a difference in the following areas all of which I have a personal story about:

1. Ending Period Poverty - locally and across the globe
2. Domestic Violence Advocacy
3. Cancer Support
4. Education

It takes courage to share personal experiences, lots of courage to be honest. I have been sharing my story since 2013 but have been trying to put it in writing for years. One of the most profound ideologies that I have recently implemented is to get rid of the "should of mentality."
Once we remove the guilt, shame, and come from behind the masks we use to hide our truths, we can share our freedom with the world. Additionally, we ignite others to be free to tell their stories, too. Sharing stories ignites transparency, and transparency ignites freedom from our raw life experiences.

Transparency breeds freedom, freedom to uplift and inspire, FREEDOM to be!
May the pain to purpose behind each arm of outreach of Giving Hope & Help ignite you to share your story. Your intentional actions will empower you to live your purpose. Also, when you work on your assignment daily, you will lift, inspire, and give hope and help to others, ultimately, becoming a world changer.

The Birth of Giving Hope & Help

The gift of speaking, heart to serve, giving hope and help to others in my DNA, as well as the survival of my life experiences that led me with the desire to found Giving Hope & Help Inc.
It was 2013, I couponed for sanitary napkins only, and loved the rush of getting them at such a great price after price matching and using coupons. I had so many in my closet, under my bed, in the linen closet etc. My daughter and I would not be able to use them all in 5 years! I knew the nonprofit I longed to start had something to do with ending period poverty. I believe, for everything you have suffered or survived there is purpose.
I began writing thoughts on Giving Hope & Help, the nonprofit I longed to start in a 70-page spiral notebook. God would literally wake me up in my sleep with ideas and what I needed to do, who I needed to contact and share my ideas with etc. One day in my closet, I looked at all of the pads I had purchased from couponing. I thought, I'll give them to friends and family for Christmas in October. I did just that and all of the recipients were so blessed and excited to receive them! Mid-October 2013, it was so heavy on my mind, wondering if domestic violence shelters needed period products. I had to pull over on the side of the road and Google local DV shelters. The first one I called; I got a voicemail. I left a message. The second one was Hope House of Jackson County, Missouri. I got a voice, I call her "The Voice" to this day. She answered my phone call. I told her who I was and let her know that I was launching a nonprofit for my 45th Thanksgiving birthday and wondered if they needed period products. She excitedly replied, "yes, we have lots of toiletries, toothpaste, shampoo/conditioner etc., but we rarely receive period products. I quickly responded, "I am going to solve that problem." I thought to myself, what

did I just say? I did not have a business plan, but I had an idea and a purpose. The moment I said, "I am going to solve that problem," she said, "would you like to come take a tour?" I replied, sure, I am on the side of the road in a parking lot. She asked where are you exactly? I told her where I was. Are you ready for this? I was literally right across the street from Hope House! I instantly knew I was being guided by God to lead me to this place, this conversation and I knew it was the beginning of an assignment that was much bigger than myself. I went over to take the tour. She showed me the pantry of toiletries that did not have any period products in it at the time. She explained that they use up to 52 rolls of toilet paper a day as the clients were making pads out of toilet paper. I assured her that they would no longer need to do that. Now, I had roughly 6 weeks to pull off fulfilling what I said I would do. I got to work! I created a flier to share on my social media and with my network. I shared the mission of Giving Hope & Help and the Thanksgiving Birthday Give, which was to end period poverty in domestic violence shelters and speak out against domestic violence, by supporting the survivors and the shelters that they resided in.

Since 2013, our mission to end period poverty and advocacy for domestic violence has expanded to 4 arms of outreach that center around the Social Drivers of Health:

1. ***Ending Period Poverty - locally and across the globe***
2. ***Domestic Violence Advocacy***
3. ***Cancer Support***
4. ***Education***

Our Mission: *Giving Hope & Help is a 501c3 nonprofit organization that supports domestic violence survivors, provides essential resources to end period poverty, empowers college bound and non-traditional students, and inspires cancer patients; lifting all those we serve to live their best life.*

We have garnered impactful partnerships and collaborations with hundreds of nonprofits, organizations, churches, schools, businesses, companies and states to move our mission.

1. <u>Feminine Hygiene Period Product Drives to End Period Poverty and promote Domestic Violence Awareness & Prevention</u>

<u>MENSTRUATION EDUCATION to Ending Period Poverty</u>

I started the mission to end period poverty in the 7th grade and had no idea that I was advocating for menstrual equity then. Plus, there wasn't even the idea for me to create a worldwide impact on girls, women and menstruators to help them through their own period experiences. Yet, that's exactly the evolution Giving Hope & Help took to create change by ending the shame, silence, physical complications, and economic concerns around period poverty and menstruation.

I learned a lot about my body and period/menstruation/cycle from experience and trial and error, not because anyone talked to me about it. There was a film in 5th grade that we watched about menstruation, but ZERO conversation from the teachers about it; no questions asked or answered by the teachers or nurse took place after the film. Menstruation was clearly viewed as shameful.

The trend of silence around menstruation continued, and I became further emboldened to create change. I remember the shame and embarrassment for girls who started their cycle at school and soiled their pants, due to lack of products/preparedness, and the silence of any instruction or education around their changing bodies. Oh, my goodness I was heartbroken and so embarrassed for them.

This powerful personal insight only furthered my commitment to period education, due to the stigma of silence surrounding a normal biological function. I was determined to change that stigma for myself and other young girls. I was the girl at school that had a pad for others and myself on PURPOSE. I was prepared with feminine products at all times, because I wasn't comfortable with the silence of "THE PERIOD" not being normalized.

My own physical complications meant very heavy periods that lasted 7-10 days, using up to 3 pads at once. I began to think about what would women do if they didn't have access, or money available, to have enough period products for themselves or other women in their family? The questions started to formulate in my mind- "What could I do to help women who couldn't afford period products?" I began to realize the economic impact created by menstruation for menstruators of all ages.

My Menstrual migraines, acne and cramping heavily existed the week before my cycle, during my cycle, and a week after my cycle. Fibroids were the culprit of excess bleeding. I was diagnosed with them as a teen. I learned to help control the symptoms with Ibuprofen and much prayer! As the years passed, managing my period and fibroids was just a normal way of life for me. The fibroids caused preterm labor with both my pregnancies, and I eventually had to have a hysterectomy at the age of 50 due to fibroid complications. Many women live with fibroids silently. So, I have lent my voice to bring awareness from experience.

I've shared all of this to drive awareness, and end the shame of period poverty, physical complications, and economic concerns by collecting and distributing period products all over the world. I have given a voice to end period poverty through my pain. If I had not had fibroids and a heavy cycle, my purpose of making a difference for thousands of women, girls and menstruators, locally and around the world, would not exist.

"For everything you have suffered and survived there is PURPOSE."
~Jessica Lynn Speaks Life

November 30, 2013, ***"The Thanksgiving Birthday Give"-Launch of Giving Hope & Help and 1st Annual Feminine Hygiene Products Drive*** was established to collect sanitary napkins and tampons. Over 5,000 products were collected to benefit the domestic violence shelter, Hope House in Jackson County, MO- 2 locations. To date, Giving Hope & Help supports 30+ domestic violence shelters/places of refuge. Texas Giving Hope & Help launched Nov. 2015, with the first annual feminine product drive.
Giving Hope & Help collects period products and packaged children and women's underwear year-round via partnerships with businesses, organizations, companies, and the community to support the NO MENSTRUATOR WITHOUT PERIOD PRODUCTS MOVEMENT. This movement benefits domestic violence survivors (and the shelters in which they live), natural disaster survivors, the unhoused community, schools, churches, women, girls/menstruators, organizations, and those in need of feminine care locally and across the globe. Since February 2020, we have hosted a FREE PERIOD PANTRY every first Saturday in collaboration with a

local church. The pantry is a blessing to the community and solves the problem of access to period products for all.

To date, Giving Hope & Help period products have landed in the hands of girls, women and menstruators in 15 countries and counting! Giving Hope & Help plans to physically go to Africa November 2024, to hand deliver 500+ reusable pads to girls and menstruators at 3 high schools! Our support to an African nonprofit, Smart Child Kenya, for the last 7 consecutive years with funding for them to make reusable pads and funding for panties has positively impacted 674 girls as of 2024. GH&H local and global impact has benefited over 50,000 women, girls. **Donations of period products have exceeded One Million!**

The mission to end period poverty and support those in need of items of dignity has expanded to supporting men as well with our LOVE Bags 4 Him - bags filled with essentials to support unhoused men, LOVE Bags 4 Her - gently used, nice and new designer purses filled with essentials and period products as well as our LOVE Bags PERIOD - bags filled with period products and our newest initiative - The LOVE Box PERIOD - a red and white, polka dot decorative box filled with organic period products, menstruation education and novelties to inspire a girl that is transitioning to womanhood. It also makes a great gift for any menstruator and is available on our website.

2. ***LOVE Bags 4 Cancer Donation & Delivery Events***

In 2015, I was inspired to launch LOVE Bags 4 Cancer in honor of my late niece, Tieara R. McCallop. Tieara was the first grandchild and my first niece. She and my sister lived with us when she was born. She was literally my live baby doll replacing the one hundred plus doll collection I had.

Tieara was a vivacious fashionista! At the age of 27 she was diagnosed with Hodgkin's Lymphoma. She fought it like a girl, woman and man for six years. Her mantra was, “Go Fight Win!” She was always in and out of the hospital on holidays and loved to do her makeup and hair even when she was battling. You could always find her in a cute outfit on her way to chemo. I wanted to do something special for her and those battling cancer in the hospital on holidays. I chose the holidays: Valentine's Day and Mother's Day. The assignment was to fill bags for males and females with inspiring items, toiletries, inspiring books and novelties to let them know that people cared about them that they did not even know. I talked to Tieara about it and just like that, LOVE Bags 4 Cancer was birthed from her pain.

"For EVERYTHING you have suffered and survived there is PURPOSE."
~Jessica Lynn Speaks Life

We launched the 1st Annual LOVE Bags 4 Cancer Donation & Delivery Event Valentine's Day 2015, with a local hospital that Tieara was released from the day before. She was able to hand deliver and inspire fellow cancer patients with the LOVE Bags 4 Cancer at the same cancer unit she was in! It was like God healed her for this special day to deliver the LOVE Bags. The next day she was readmitted to the same unit. She fought long and strong for 6 years before she transitioned to heaven at the young age of 34, Oct. 2, 2016. Today, in her honor, we have uplifted and inspired over 700 cancer patients with a LOVE BAG 4 Cancer. A portion of the proceeds from the LOVE Bags 4 Cancer Donation & Delivery events benefits the American Cancer Society of Kansas City.

GH&H also co-hosts a breast cancer brunch for those battling or who have survived breast cancer. Over 60 women of color breast cancer survivors in the KC Metro have been honored since 2021 and have received a LOVE Bags 4 Cancer.

3. *Education Is Your Passport Program (EIYP)/Scholarship Program*

In 2015, the Education Is Your Passport initiative was birthed from my college life experiences and the pain and determination of my ancestors, great- great grandparents who were slaves, great- grandparents, grandparents and parents.

My great-great grandfather, Harrison McCallop Sr. was a slave in Tennessee. He fought in the Civil War in 1863, at the age of 15 and was a decorated soldier. After gaining his freedom he and my great-great grandmother, Nellie (Jackson) McClallop moved to Shawnee, Kansas in

Johnson County to farm. They had 14 children and desired for all of them to be educated. They knew education was the passport out of poverty and that it also led to freedom and equality. Unfortunately, their children were not granted the right to a full public education in Johnson County because they were African American/Black. Their 14th child, Robert Lee McCallop Sr., was my great-grandfather, whom I grew up with. My great-great grandfather Harrison taught my great-grandfather, Robert, to farm. They provided produce to the community. The very community that they were not allowed to be educated in because of the color of their skin.

My earliest memories are of Grandpa Robert and grandma babysitting me after kindergarten. I went to Flint Elementary School in Shawnee for Kindergarten, with my two older sisters. Since I was dismissed earlier than them, I would walk to my great-grandparents house across the street until my mom would come get me. I was blessed to have Grandpa Robert until I was 12 years old. He was a strong leader with an amazing character, very intelligent and business minded, even though he did not receive a full education.

Grandpa Robert and my great grandma Mary, had 5 children, Alexander Harrison McCallop Sr. was their son and also my grandfather, my father's father. The dream of their children receiving a full public education was carried on with them even though neither of them nor their parents had the opportunity to receive one.

"For EVERYTHING you have suffered and survived there is PURPOSE." ~Jessica Lynn Speaks Life

Grandpa Robert had a third-grade education. He wanted his children and his grandchildren, me, to be educated. So, he provided a solution for his children and other black children in Johnson County, Kansas.

Grandpa Robert's solution was to transform his agricultural truck into a bus to transport black children from Johnson County to Wyandotte County, Kansas. They would pass 5 white high schools before they would reach one that would accept them because of the color of their skin. That school was Sumner Academy High School. My grandfather, Alexander, and many family members graduated from there. The McCallop Bus Company, founded by my great-grandfather, Robert, was the first bus company founded in Shawnee Kansas/Johnson County. It ended up with a fleet of 14 buses. The company ran for over 35 years.

Grandpa Robert was a Christian man that instilled Christian values into his children. He was a trailblazer, humanitarian, and change-maker that provided inroads and transportation for children of color to receive a full public education. He is pictured on the mural of the Shawnee City Hall. My grandparents and The McCallop Bus Co. are permanently and prominently featured with a dedicated exhibit at the Johnson County Museum in Johnson County, Kansas for their contributions to racial equality and providing inroads to education for students of color.

February 23, 2021, the Mayor of Shawnee Kansas, who learned about my Grandpa Robert when she was in the 4th grade in public school in Shawnee, Kansas ordered this day to be McCallop Family Day.

Today, I and many of my cousins and family members hold professional degrees, are business owners, lawyers, doctors etc. We are literally our ancestors and grandparents' wildest dreams!

"The McCallop legacy - from slavery to school buses, to scholarships and service to all mankind."

I was a scholar throughout elementary and high school. I earned an internship with INROADS Kansas City, Inc. while in high school and worked the internship in corporate America throughout college. Upon high school graduation, I was awarded a full ride, a Presidential Scholarship to a small historical black college, Texas College in Tyler, Texas. After successfully completing my first year with a 3.8 GPA and 33 credit hours I wanted to transfer to a larger HBCU, Southern University and Agricultural College in Baton Rouge, Louisiana. The problem was that the scholarship/funding was not transferable. My parents did not have the finances to support me, so I packed my bags and flew to Louisiana for the first time with $125 in my purse. I found myself waiting in a SIX HOUR financial aid line at Southern University, only to discover that I was in the wrong line once it was my turn after six hours. The dream to fund scholarships was ignited in me as I waited in that 6-hour line. I wanted to pay for myself and everyone that was in line with me! Four years later, I graduated with honors. However, if I had not transferred from the "all expenses paid" college, Texas College, and waited in that grueling six-hour line, my purpose to award scholarships to students would not exist. The Education Is Your Passport Program was literally born from my DNA and college life experiences.

I am honored to carry on the legacy of education with the arm of outreach: Education Is Your Passport. The mission of the program is to provide educational and financial assistance for Pre-K through adult college and non-traditional students. The program's annual scholarship initiative: **The Education Is Your Passport Scholarship Program**, benefits underserved high school seniors and non-traditional, college bound students with cash scholarships, tools and resources to attend and graduate college.

The program awards 5 cash scholarships: Two HBCU (Historically Black College and University) Scholarships, A Perseverance Award Scholarship, and two scholarships in my grandparents' honor: The Neoma Spearman Literary Scholarship. She was my hero. One cash scholarship in my paternal grandparents' honor: The Alexander Sr. and Cleo McCallop Legacy of Giving Scholarship.

Since the scholarship program's 2015 launch we have awarded 126 college scholarships including 6 FULL RIDE SCHOLARSHIPS to Metropolitan Community College-Penn Valley, valued at $418,000.

"For EVERYTHING you have suffered and survived there is PURPOSE."
~Jessica Lynn Speaks Life

4. A Way of Escape from Domestic Violence Initiative (AWOE)- Launched June 2023

The life-saving purpose of the A Way of Escape from Domestic Violence Initiative is to aide KC metro area women, clients, and residents of domestic violence shelters in the KC metro area with funding and resources to EQUIP, EMPOWER and provide "A Way of ESCAPE from

Domestic Violence", leading them to live life to their fullest potential free of violence and abuse.

In our first year we exhausted $60,500 to support 30 women with this initiative. We partnered with local domestic violence agencies to provide resources to support women to live a life free from domestic violence in the following ways:

- Transportation
- Rent
- Utilities
- Safe Stays at Hotels

This initiative was inspired not only by my personal pain and decision to leave a toxic emotionally violent relationship, but also by others that have suffered from domestic violence. Some, unfortunately, did not survive. I am thinking of my dear friend, cousin and countless souls who lost her lives due to domestic violence. If you see something wrong, say something. It is our responsibility to be there for eachother. It takes all of us. Together we can break the cycle of abuse.

"For EVERYTHING you have suffered and survived there is PURPOSE."
~Jessica Lynn Speaks Life

I hope Giving Hope & Help ignites you to become an agent of social change.

When you work your assignment and purpose daily, you will lift, inspire, and give hope and help to others, ultimately, being a world changer. Your raw life experiences, good or bad, have purpose. The impact of your story, that is derived from everything you have suffered and survived, can be the support for others to feel less alone in their journey. Your purpose is directly connected to someone else's destiny to live life in freedom. GH&H and I encourage you to share your story. We would love to hear it. Remember, transparency breeds freedom, freedom to uplift and inspire, FREEDOM to be!

Jessica Lynn McCallop-McClellan is an inspirational speaker, (Jessica Lynn Speaks Life), and Christian minister. Her mantra is: "I Live to Give." She's been an impactful keynote speaker in corporate America, women's events, and inspirational movements. As the Founder and President of 501c3, nonprofit organization, Giving Hope & Help Inc., founded in 2013. One of her purposes is to speak for the voiceless and inspire others to find their voice and use it for change. She is a "Voice for the Voiceless", survivor and advocate for domestic violence and sexual assault survivors, menstrual equity, education, cancer support advocate, humanitarian, philanthropist, voice for equality and justice, founder and administrator of the Black, Brown and White UNITE for CHANGE Facebook Group. She has eight years experience as the radio/internet talk show host - Jessica Lynn Speaks Life on KUAW Radio, Kansas City's Global Community Radio Internet Radio Show. Jessica has received many prestigious awards and recognitions for her philanthropic work, humanitarianism, and leadership in the community and with Giving Hope & Help Inc., (GH&H). She has been featured in media, podcasts, magazines, and television many times for the difference and impact she and the organization are making in the community and across the globe. She is a 1st generation graduate from HBCU- Southern University and A&M College – Baton Rouge, LA, where she earned a Bachelor of Science in Business Marketing. She also holds a Master of Science in Business Management (MSM) from Baker University – Baldwin City, KS. Jessica has over twenty-nine years of sales and management experience including ten years of pharmaceutical and medical sales experience. She is an Independent Corporate Trainer/Facilitator; a volunteer and leader of many organizations. Jessica resides in Kansas City, Missouri with her husband, Kevin of 27 years. She loves spending time with him, her two adult children, grandchildren and family. She is empowered by her favorite Bible scriptures: Proverbs 3:5-6, Philippians 4:13 and Jer. 29:11.

Giving Hope & Help Inc.

Vision

Giving Hope & Help values and acts upon the opportunity to provide hope and help for every person to pursue happiness, health, wealth and education via the avenues, fundraisers and support offered by the organization.

Core Values

Gratitude- to be grateful for the opportunity to make an impact in others' lives.

Inspire hearts to give and make a difference.

Voice - to give a voice to the voiceless.

Equity, **E**quality and **E**xcellence – in giving to ALL.

Giving Hope & Help Inc. PO Box 2446 - Lee's Summit, Missouri 64063

*Phone: 816-607-1813

*Email: donate@givinghopeandhelp.com

*Website: www.givinghopeandhelp.org

www.facebook.com/givinghopeandhelp www.twitter.com/givehopehelp www.instagram.com/givehopehelp

YouTube: Giving Hope & Help LinkedIn

Jessica Lynn McClellan - Facebook

Black Brown White Unite for CHANGE - Facebook

LinkedIn - Jessica McClellan, MSM

JessicaLynnSpeaksLife@gmail.com

FROM SHADOWS TO SUNLIGHT - FINDING LIGHT IN THE DARKNESS OF GROWTH

First off, what an incredible gift this opportunity is to share some parts of my life story within the pages of my friend Caroline Markel's book. The timing of this gift is perfect as I am at the time in my life where I am learning to express myself in the most emotionally mature way that I am currently capable of, and it has everything to do with my layers of transformation that have taken place over the last 12 years.

Without me knowing that my transformation was under way, it was all ignited with the darkest moment I had ever been through. The sudden death of my older brother. At the time, he was 29 and I was 27. It was a Saturday, October 22, 2011. I had come home to my 3-flat apartment in a northside neighborhood in Chicago. I fed my cats, stripped off my scrubs, put on a big t-shirt and was about to crawl back into bed for my typical after-work-Saturday-nap. Nothing got in the way of my napping hobby, my escape from reality. Especially phone calls, it didn't matter who it was, even if it was my mom, because she loved to talk... and there she was, my mom, calling me... any other day I would have let it go to voicemail. Not that day. I 'knew' to answer. "Hi mom." "Courtney." "Yeah?" "Come to my house." "......okay." This was the shortest exchange of words on a call we've ever had. She never greeted me in that way, it was always "Hi honey, it's just me!" Everything in her energy told me something had happened, even before I answered the phone.

Apparently, my older brother, Brett, was feeling pretty sick for a couple of days. He was living with my Mom and younger brother Chad who had both told him to get checked out. Brett was like many of us when told what to do, stubborn to do just the opposite. Turns out, a few other people told him to seek medical attention as he was on his way to work that day. Brett was a natural performer and expressed his gifts in a myriad of ways throughout his life: musician, singer, cashier at Jewel, pharmacy tech; and at the time: event DJ, bartender, sketch comic. On this particular day, he was DJing a wedding in Schaumburg, IL. As he was setting up for this wedding, from what we've been told, he had come out of an elevator at the hotel, carrying a DJ table skirt, he laid the black cloth down and then laid down on top of it. A hotel worker witnessed this and thought Brett was some drunk guy, but as he walked closer to Brett, he saw his face was blue, so he ran out to the crowd of wedding attendees and called out for a doctor. A doctor and nurse couple ran to Brett... he was already in rigor mortis. As a healthcare worker, I knew biologically, that meant that there was no longer an opportunity to revive him.

On that Saturday, pretty sure every relative we have in Illinois came to my Mom's home. And at one point during the night, my Mom came to Chad and I and said that we had to go to my Dad's house to tell him Brett died. It had been a few years since I spoke to my Dad. And it had actually been even longer since I had an actual conversation with Brett. That's how I used to be, if there were differing opinions, or if I felt misunderstood time and time again with someone, I'd avoid addressing the issue and just turn away. I'd blame them, talk shit about them, resent them and basically hold on to all the negative emotions I had connected to the string of situations that happened. Now you might have a better understanding of what I meant when I said "emotionally mature" at the beginning of all this.

I don't remember which of us drove, but I do remember the three of us walking hand in hand up to the front door of the house we all shared for the first 20 years of my life. My Mom told my Dad and then I saw my Dad express his pain in a way I had never witnessed anyone express anything ever before. At that moment, we were all so connected. So in the moment, there was no time to think or hide who we really were. We were all in pain and the years of practice of disconnecting and turning away from pain didn't matter. Miraculously, my sister and brother, my Dad's two kids from his first marriage were both in town from Florida for the first time in 10 years. They weren't there at the moment, but it gave me a lot of comfort that my Dad wasn't going to be alone after we left. My wall of resentment softened that day. A seed was planted for my future layer of transformation.

It took several weeks for the autopsy results to show that pneumonia was the "cause" of his death. Now I know that all of our lives end from the same thing, loss of oxygen, it's just a matter of which path takes us there. My science-driven brain took in a lot of what the medical examiner shared with my Mom, Chad and me. I went down a number of rabbit holes to find answers... "what causes pneumonia", "what is the immune system", "what is gut health". Those rabbit holes of new learnings were quickly filled in with all my habits at the time: weekends of red wine, partying, sleeping, closet smoking, guilt, grief, questioning my existence, all the while working a new job and having the chance to work overtime for the first time as an adult, and so I did. I had been dating my new boyfriend for about four months when Brett died. It was my first long-distance relationship.

Six months later my boyfriend moved to Chicago. It then became clear to me that his daily habits were exactly like my weekend habits. The escape from reality continued for months until I just couldn't keep up anymore, I felt disgusting physically, mentally, and emotionally. I would tell him that I can't party anymore and that we have to change. So, we'd go on a break from drinking and fast food, he would last a week and come home drunk. Then I'd have the same conversation. Then the break would last a few weeks for him. So, I thought there was a trend in the right direction. Then there'd be "stress", and "panic attacks", and the whiskey would come out from hiding. He'd go out and then drive home. I'd get so frustrated. My voice would go from talking, to sobbing to telling him I felt like I was going crazy saying the same things all the time. And he would tell me to "get that crazy checked out". I felt obsessed. And I was definitely overanalyzing his choices, like he was holding up an invisible mirror for me to see the direction of my future. But at that time, I thought it was just a rough time in our lives and I had hoped that it could only get better. I knew he was a good person, but I also knew there was some deep pain that he was avoiding because I saw people in my family with the same habits.

He asked me to marry him, and I told him before we got married that if he couldn't choose me over drinking that our marriage wouldn't last. He told me he understood. With the wedding ahead, my goals became: I don't want to be a bride lighting up a cigarette in my wedding dress, so I have to quit smoking aaaand of course, start working out. I started the P90X DVDs at home and got down to only a few cigarettes a day. He floated in and out of the same patterns, some moments better, some moments worse. My hope remained. The wedding came, and it really was a positive day. After the wedding vibes simmered back to normalcy, not much changed in our lives except where we lived, his job from bartender to liquor rep and the increased space between our emotions. Autopilot set in, patterns repeated, life was life.

There came a day where I was in our master bath, peeing on a stick, waiting for the results... Negative. I laid my head back on the wall behind the toilet and relief poured over me. I remember scrunching my face in confusion, I wanted so badly to be a mom. I dreamt of having four kids for as long as I could remember. Why was I relieved that I *wasn't* pregnant? Hard to explain this because I didn't exactly hear anything...but this feeling of "this isn't the way" came over me. The seed of my transformation was watered by that feeling.

I walked out into our living room. He was sitting there staring outside, the sunset glowing over the grass in our front yard, petting our black lab with his left hand, holding a glass of whiskey on the rocks in his right. And I said "you know that crazy you're always telling me to get checked out, I'm going to go. And you can either come with me or just be ready for what's to come when I get back." After processing my words, and asking me a few clarifying questions, he said he'd go with me.

The search for a counselor felt like my life depended on it and it was pretty overwhelming considering who was within my insurance, close enough, targeted their services toward couples, and had kind eyes, they had to have kind eyes. I found her. Our counseling sessions were nothing short of emotional. The first handful began with mostly tears, barely any words and gradually transformed into me admitting to this overwhelming disappointment and disconnect from love and life. I divulged my craving for more depth and connection but questioned if it was even possible.

My counselor asked me questions to encourage me to see my life from a different perspective and the more I put my feelings into words and released them from within me, the more I realized I was blaming him (and everyone around me) for the way I felt. I complained constantly, I wasn't taking any responsibility, I had zero self-esteem, I avoided all conflicts until it boiled up within me. I became the person I never wanted to be. I saw these patterns as I grew up and became the exact person I feared becoming. I saw that I was so focused on not becoming this person that I focused on no one else to become.

The more I shared, the more I remembered happy daydreams that I had had throughout life, and I also remembered them disappearing with doubt and shame. Like my own thoughts crushed my own dreams. My counselor would recommend YouTube videos to watch from Brene Brown and books to read by Byron Katie. She suggested a support group for family members of people with substance habits. I went, I met other people who grew up in homes like I did. There was love and affection, but it was often overshadowed by tension and emotional disconnect. This was the result of generational trauma that was rooted from a lack of emotional support from their parents who grew up in generations like the Great Depression.

My teenage resentment toward my parents for unhappily staying together softened into empathy and understanding. I grew to see that they did their absolute best with their circumstances at the time. I can only imagine that if I did get pregnant how life would have carried on in a similar fashion. I was given the chance to elevate my life just as they had clearly made choices to elevate their lives compared to the lives their parents lived. I, of course, couldn't comprehend any of that as a child. And I now see that these situations, circumstances, conditions can all provide clarity to choosing a different path. This awareness was like sunshine on the seed of my future layers of transformation.

I allowed in concepts that I had heard before, but prior to this point, I just wasn't emotionally mature enough to let in. Like the concept that I couldn't control anyone other than myself and my only responsibility was to control my responses. And taking responsibility for my own actions, responsibility for my own happiness, it wasn't until I disrupted my patterns with this counseling, and the resources shared with me there and then this support group did I see that I was blaming everyone around me for the problems in my life.

There was another hard to explain moment during a counseling session where it basically felt like I was looking in from the upper corner of the room, I saw myself and my husband sitting next to each other as we had for the last year. There was a brightness about me, an enthusiasm, an eagerness and I believed this to be confirmation that I was ready to choose the path of growth. The seedling of my transformation was watered. I didn't want to choose to stay where I was, stuck in my tornado thoughts, stuck in this marriage, stuck in a dull life. I had asked him multiple times what he wanted, and he would say he wanted the same as me, but his actions did not change from years prior. Going into counseling, I was confused, conflicted and uncertain. Over months of learning, growing and contributing, it became clear to me that I was ready to part ways. Our focus and values no longer matched. They did for all the reasons they did, and it took time, but I am now very grateful for the clarity and lessons I experienced within that relationship.

With the divorce underway, space opened within my mind for me. My health moved up my priority list. The new routine was my job, the gym, and dating with the mindset to practice who I wanted to be for myself and in a relationship. I was trying to adjust to new management at the office for over a year. A lot of changes were happening at the office, and I'd love to say that I was optimistic about the shifts, but I'll be real - I wasn't. I talked about my job a lot in counseling. About how it was pretty much what I had dreamed about since I graduated from my dental hygiene program in 2009. It was the specialty I wanted to work in, but even more, I was asked to help create a new position to support the main surgeon after his partner of 20 years had just retired. Not only did I get to provide advanced clinical care, but I got to provide advanced education to patients as well. I felt special, I felt needed, I felt secure. But with the shift in focus under new management, my attitude reflected frustration, stress and immaturity.

I have struggled with anxious feelings for as long as I can remember. And I let it keep me from using my voice in constructive ways. I'd mostly complain constantly behind closed doors or emotionally snap in moments of pressure when I felt unheard or misunderstood. So, this situation at work triggered a lot of these patterns within me. I turned to the gym to let out some of this frustration. I put in the work and the result was that I was in the best physical shape I had ever been. I felt amazing and strong in so many ways! But I also still felt so disconnected, like anywhere I went, I didn't belong. It's like I had taken great strides forward in my life, but still felt held back emotionally, mentally and physically.

I had been dealing with a strange pressure pain in my lower legs for some time. I thought it was a circulation problem since varicose veins ran in my family. I finally got the courage to see a doctor about it, was referred to a few different specialists, went through basic tests, bloodwork, physical exams, then had my first MRI, CT scan, ultrasounds on my legs. It was months and thousands of dollars with "nothing" found anywhere.

The feeling of frustration felt like a constant program just running in my background. The physical pains felt while working, the mental pains of anxiety felt while working, and the emotional pains of feeling I didn't belong came to a boiling point for me. Another hard-to-explain moment happened at work while I was sitting at my desk. My imagination (or intuition) brought this visualization to my mind, I saw wings sprouting from my back, breaking free from my skin and clothes, expanding beyond the walls of the small office I was in, enabling me to fly free. My future transformation continued to be watered.

Not long after this, a fear that I was being replaced at my job came true. I was fired. The reason wasn't completely accurate, but I was so tired of pushing the blame and just living in this state of irritability, I actually felt relief. Relief, like when I found out I wasn't pregnant. Relief, like I didn't have to play that part that I didn't want to play anymore anyway. Relief to fly free. I sat in my car in the parking lot outside the building I had worked in for six years. I realized just as I felt powerless in my last relationship, I ran the same pattern with my job. I learned that connecting these dots was growing my awareness, which was key to shifting my mindset.

With this next chapter of life, my anxious feelings were swirling around. I was putting a lot of the tools I had been learning in counseling to use walking in nature, conscious breathing, hanging with my cats, reading self-improvement, and jotting down thoughts here and there. I was reading an article about anxiety and noticed an ad about the food-mood connection. I asked my counselor about this food-mood connection. I told her that I kind of assumed antianxiety and antidepressant medications were inevitable since the majority of my patients were taking them. I wasn't against medications, but I was curious what other options were out there. That was one of the best insights I had learned from the surgeon I just got fired from, hehe. He empowered all of his patients to ask questions, ask about alternatives and seek a second opinion to gain clarity before making decisions. He shared this repeatedly and it made me realize how rarely I asked questions and how rarely I felt clarity. My counselor shared that medications are an option, along with understanding the brain-gut correlation and she encouraged me to use my science-drive to dig into learning. My search brought me back to my hunt for answers after Brett died... And just like those rabbit holes filled in back then, a few other pressing matters came to the forefront, like finding a job... and meeting Joe...

It almost felt like I was practicing becoming me with everyone I met, before meeting Joe. I refined my standards and manifested my ideal self. His willingness to be real, and go to a depth in conversation most guys I was meeting would deflect really drew me in. After weeks of getting to know each other, we developed a level of trust that allowed me to be honest with myself and him. I shared with him how far I had come but how I also still felt lost… in my career, in my body, in my mind. He had this passion in his energy and was actually excited! Which was strange to me, but intriguing. He asked me a bunch of questions about why I got into dental hygiene, if there was anything else I wanted to do, what kind of impact I wanted to make, and it literally shifted the energy inside me from fear to curiosity. He talked about self-development and shared some audio tracks with me to help support my mindset. The line that my mind highlighted from all that he shared was “the most expensive thing you can have is a closed mind, so be open to all opportunities, you never know what they can lead you to”. It felt like my transformation seed was fed with the best dose of water and sunshine!

Joe’s impact question brought me back to Brett’s wake… The number of times people told my Mom, Chad, me and anyone standing there, how Brett “impacted” their life *really* imprinted on my long term memory bank. The line of people waiting their turn to “pay their respects” to Brett and us, his family, seemed to be never ending. All day, and all night, the line was out the door of the funeral home building. Then it began to rain, and the line of amazing people continued. Then police had to direct traffic for people entering and leaving the funeral home parking lot! Every story shared by these individuals made us laugh, made us cry and made us so incredibly grateful to know this one human that positively influenced *so* many others!

Deciphering these people’s stories and thinking deeper about this experience of hearing the impact of Brett in all these lives unraveled another layer of myself. I got into health care to help people. Brett helped what seemed to be thousands of lives, maybe more, feel something meaningful, that they mattered. And when Brett and I were close, he made me feel that way too. I started to realize that I was jealous of his ability to connect with others, his bravery to be real, and the way he accepted people as they were without worrying what they thought of him. I was stuck in my own head, behind so many fears, which kept me from stretching outside of my comfort to communicate with others and feel that level of connection I had longed for. And it's not like it was an easy road for him either, the more I analyzed Brett's life, the more I realized that he pushed through the greatest amounts of rejection since his early years, to find his people. Those that received the wonderful, natural gifts he was born to share. That's what I wanted to do.

One of my many fears was the fear of looking dumb, especially in front of a partner. And this fear would end up limiting me and again the connection I craved. But opening up to Joe like I had, and his energetic responses positively confirmed that with the right support, I can grow through my limiting patterns. Clarity surfaced about the person I wished to be and be with in a relationship. Everything felt distinctly unique about us. The progression in my relationship with Joe amplified my own self-image in the mirror. He opened my eyes to the realm of possibility and having my own business. With Joe's unwavering support over the next year through multiple career opportunities, I began to consider the prospect of running my own health and well-being franchise. I jumped past a bajillion fears and went for it. With this leap came an entirely new environment of people all focused on health in every aspect, physically, mentally, emotionally and spiritually. Learning from these leaders, I went through a health transformation that was nothing short of a revelation.

I had my very own experience of the very subjects that were seeded into my consciousness through Brett's medical examiner 7 years earlier and then again by my counselor only two years before. The brain-gut connection. How food affected my mental health, but also my hormones, my focus, my digestion issues, my immune system, my metabolism! Obviously, everyone's experience is their own experience. Mine was filled with a consistent higher mood, less tornado thoughts/anxiety, less triggers that would turn on my irritability, mood swings, resentment, holding grudges that would just plain distract me from what I wanted to focus on and who I wanted to be. Not to mention the turnaround on my chronic IBS (for me it was bloating and constipation), migraines, headaches, face and body acne, acid reflux, addiction to coffee and lunch-time naps. Oh, and remember that weird leg pressure pain - gone. I had my power back within my body, within my mind, and within my career. We've all heard the phrase "You are what you eat", but it's actually more like, we are what we absorb. I was foreign to the quality of ingredients, what comes from nature and what works with our bodies. I've learned that inflammatory foods (and inflammatory thoughts) are clouding people. When we take a break from them, the body wakes up, the systems within us communicate properly and we begin to heal. In the right environment, we all can heal.

I now work with people who are looking to raise their standards with their health, vitality and wellbeing. I really appreciate this definition of *health*: the freedom of having to think about it, right?? Because health really is wealth. If we don't have our health, we invest 100% of our energy, time, and eventually money to try to get it back. So how do we raise our standards in our health? To be honest, it's pretty simple... if we don't have the level of health & vitality right now that we wish... it's due to our environment & mindset. Wellness is a path we will forever be on until we stop breathing. It's a journey! There will be variables constantly! It's about who we become on this path. Our growth and our contributions.

Wellbeing to me is waking up now at age 40 & not aching, it's the energy to make food rather than stopping at Starbucks, it's regulating my mood and not snapping at people, it's the willingness to invest in feeling alive and connected to everyone in my life. It's feeling fulfilled.

I've learned after being a wellbeing consultant for 5 years that there's a missing link for many. We start with awareness, then shift to inspiration, motivation, then action... something happens... where's the final link to lasting positive change? It's in our identity. As you may have gathered by now, my identity has evolved in what feels like 360 degrees. Our identity is created by our beliefs, our habits and who we spend the most time with. Without us realizing it, our identity attempts to evolve and grow. Sometimes it's our thoughts and old patterns that are resisting that growth. Those of us who let go of control and surrender then become uniquely qualified to help the people going through the same struggles and experiences as we did. Just as so many supported me through my struggles and growth moments, I am sharing that gift of love forward. One of the most profound realizations for me has been that pain is inevitable, but resistance and suffering is a choice, and I am choosing differently. This understanding, embodied and brought to light by my brother Brett, has greatly influenced the way I frame my world.

I also collaborate, train and mentor other wellbeing enthusiasts in creating their own unique impact with their own business franchise. This opportunity to step into a leadership role has led me to a much higher understanding of health and wellbeing. I've been well acquainted with pain, and now, I've grown familiar with fears and how to move through them. Having a business is one of the best forms of therapy! I've learned the amazing flexibility of the human mind and even more, the limitlessness to which the strength of the human spirit can stretch. We can all accomplish this so much more profoundly together, connected, collaboratively.

The reconnection of the body to the mind was a gift I was only ready to receive at the exact time that I was. Some amazing forces were at work along my path, planting seeds, watering them, connecting dots, creating synchronicities. I'm just deeply grateful that I woke up enough when I did to give those signs and messages the attention to receive the transformation that I have and that I believe will only continue as I choose to share my natural gifts with the world.

I've learned and now believe with all the energy within my being that we as living beings are profoundly connected to each other, are a part of nature and are a part of something so much bigger than just ourselves. And the more connected we become to our own self, the more we can positively impact each other. I believe we are here to learn, grow and contribute.

Who knew the wallflower within me would bloom into the truest most beautiful tree? I sure didn't! And now I know I wasn't supposed to. It really is about the journey and not the destination. Thank you to those who showered me along the way, humans and angels.

PS - Joe introduced me to Caroline in Riviera Maya at a Dave Matthews & Tim Reynolds 3-night concert on the beach. Joe and I had been together for 6 months at that point. It felt like Caroline had a magnet for my soul. And she still does. I love you, Caroline. Thank you for being one of the most amazing life mentors. Your example and invitation to live life on purpose has been truly life transformative for me.

Courtney Beth Anderson is a collaborative wellbeing and business trainer who imperfectly transitioned from a 20-year career in oral healthcare to a vibrant pursuit of holistic health. Her personal journey of transformation has fueled her passion, and with six years of experience, she genuinely guides individuals toward their health and wealth goals.

As an Independent Consultant with a holistic health and wellness brand, Courtney is dedicated to helping clients navigate their wellness journeys. Her mission is to empower people to thrive through sustainable wellbeing. She champions a community of entrepreneurs where wellness is a lifestyle and uplifting others reveals life's deeper meaning. Courtney's philosophy marries clean ingredients, conscious ethical and ecological practices, and an exceptional support system led by committed leaders.
Her relatable approach has empowered hundreds to achieve sustainable wellness and realize their health aspirations, while also supporting other wellbeing leaders to scale their businesses into globally impactful organizations.

Outside of her professional pursuits, Courtney is an avid nature lover, enjoying adventures with her life partner and his teenage son in the suburbs of Chicago. She finds inspiration and creativity through mind+body movement as she practices Steel Mace Flow or chases after her 3 year old niece. Tune in to her podcast The Magical Midlife Crisis where she collaborates with her best friend/business partner/co-host to feature all kinds of kinds with their perspectives of a dark turn that allowed them to find the lessons into the light of life.

Facebook: Courtney Beth Anderson
Instagram: @coco.compassion
Email: cleangreenlifer@gmail.com
Podcast: The Magical Midlife Crisis

THE SIREN SONG OF VULNERABILITY

I grew up in the Midwest, where people tend to marry young and single women over the age of 30 are considered 'old maids.' It's been this way, especially in my hometown of St. Louis since my Mom was a little girl. Couples wouldn't wait long to tie the knot, and women often felt pressured to find a husband so they could finally 'start their lives' and pop out babies. Missouri is also a state where domestic violence runs rampant, and since it's a very Catholic state, it's not uncommon for women or men to avoid divorce at all costs, staying trapped in unhappy marriages.

I wish I could say all of this was context I understood as a kid, as I listened to my Dad emotionally abuse my Mom every day, wondering how they ever wound up together in the first place. I love my Dad, but I could never understand why everything that went wrong somehow ended up being her 'fault.' As I grew older, I'd attempt to defend my Mom during these arguments, but I also learned quickly how nothing I said would make a difference. He would find reasons to blame her, and she wouldn't do anything to stop him.

My Mother was in a vulnerable state of mind as she watched all of her friends get married and start their lives. She felt pressured to marry my Dad and hoped that everything would just work out. My Mom is the most giving, selfless, kind, and loving person I know, and at this point in her life, she was incredibly vulnerable. While vulnerability is a beautiful thing that can open so many emotional doors, what we need to be careful about is who we are with when we choose to open those doors. When we are vulnerable, it's almost like we sound off a siren that only narcissists can hear. And if you're a nice person who exudes empathy, that siren is twice as loud.

I take after my Mom in a lot of ways, but my siren song of vulnerability sounded a bit different than hers. It wasn't until I got fired for the first time in my life that I reached this point. I've always thrown myself into whatever job I'm doing, and this one was very exciting to me. Until it wasn't.

"Maybe you just don't have what it takes to survive in this business," said my boss during one of our many late nights at the office.

The very next day, they let me go, for reasons I will never understand. Granted, the career path I chose was in one of the most cutthroat fields - Public Relations. PR Agencies have incredibly high turnover rates and unless you're a VP or someone in upper-level management, you'll be worked to the bone and likely suffer from burn-out. I had worked at several PR agencies at this point, representing dozens of large B2B companies and brands in the financial services sector. This agency was much different than the others. I was still working very long hours, but here, I was representing cannabis brands. I absolutely loved my clientele of edible companies, vape technology brands, etc. I threw myself into pitching journalists to cover my clients just as the Farm Bill passed in 2018 making hemp federally legal in the U.S.

The day after I was let go, I woke up to missed calls and texts from the clients I was working with, wondering if they did anything wrong to cause me to leave the company. I tried to keep my composure as I explained that my leaving wasn't by choice. I felt so humbled by the fact that every single one of them either called or texted me to check in. They sounded just as surprised as I was, which in my mind confirmed that I was actually doing a good job. At least, in the clients' eyes I was.

As a publicist, media relations have always been an important part of my job. It's also my favorite part. I enjoy the thrill of seeing articles finally published after putting in so much time researching timely news angles, gathering all of the facts, setting up interviews with clients, etc. Sometimes all of that work can result in absolutely nothing - but other times you end up with a great news story featuring your client.

I also love helping journalists do their jobs and tell stories that need to be told. Reporters play a crucial role in our society, but most media publications these days are severely understaffed and don't have funds to pay writers nearly what they deserve. Essentially, if I can make their job a little easier by connecting them to the right source for a quote or fact-checking a few statistics, I do it.

At this point, I had made lots of journalist friends in the cannabis industry, many of whom I was on a texting basis with. So when I got a text from Roger, one of my favorite writers, about a client story he was working on, I opened up and shared the unfortunate news.

Several days later, Roger gave me a call to ask me a question that I had never been asked before. It was a question that would change my career path and my life overall as I knew it.

"How much would you charge to write a one-off press release for someone, like on a freelance basis? Is that something you could do?"

It took me by surprise. Freelancing? I liked the sound of that. The idea had never crossed my mind, but I quickly replied,

"Sure! I'd have no problem throwing something together on my own."

It felt amazing to say out loud what I knew to be true but had never once considered. Even though this was completely new, I was intrigued, so I decided to take Roger up on his offer and meet with the guy looking for PR help. Little did I know this decision would change me, in a bigger way than I ever expected.

During my first call with my abuser- let's call him J, I felt nervous, excited, and most importantly, incredibly vulnerable. This led me to make several crucial mistakes during our first conversation. He had been talking about his cannabis recruiting company, claiming he wanted to help people find their passion in the cannabis industry by connecting them with credible and trustworthy employers. Still so raw and upset by what had just happened to me, I opened up about why the reporter was kind enough to introduce us- he was helping me out during a difficult time. In hindsight, I couldn't have made it any easier for J to take advantage of my situation. We quickly came up with the idea to barter services. I agreed to write the press release for free if he agreed to help me find a job. As you can probably guess, I fulfilled my end of the deal. But J never ended up finding me a job- not a full-time job anyway.

We were about a month in when I started to question whether or not he was going to hold up his end of the bargain. Whenever I brought up payment via text or email, his move was always to call me and question my commitment to what we had agreed upon. I got to a point where I would dread answering his calls, so I started the job hunt myself as I became more and more doubtful of how much I could (and should) trust his word.

I was in the midst of planning a trip to California to check out Coachella with a few friends when I decided that I needed to end things with J and move on. J was based in Los Angeles and had been begging me to visit, so we set up a time to meet in person. I had every intention of breaking things off face-to-face. My gut was telling me something wasn't right about J, and I knew it needed to be over. Little did I know, everything about our relationship was about to change.

It didn't take long before my business visit to LA started to feel more like a rom-com love montage. He showed me around town, took me out to nice dinners, the whole nine yards. Slowly but surely, the version of J that made my blood boil over the phone began to fade. Then one evening, we were sitting on his couch, and I could feel him get closer and closer to me. The nature of our relationship completely flipped, and I remember feeling my stomach drop. I didn't like it, but I decided to ignore the weird feeling in my gut telling me that something wrong was about to happen. His face inched closer and closer to mine and instead of recognizing my feelings and pulling away, making things uncomfortable, we kissed. The sparks flew.

It was at that moment I had given up any type of power that I thought I had in our previously strictly professional relationship. While this loss of power is so obvious to me now, at the moment it couldn't have felt more like the opposite. I felt a surge of confidence as confessions poured out about how impressed he was with me from the very start, and how I had done such an amazing job all on my own. Even though J failed to mention any of this before, I clung to his every encouraging word. He painted this pretty picture in my head of what it would be like for me to run my own business. This vision and all of his carefully articulated words of encouragement quickly outweighed any doubts I had about his genuineness.

It didn't take long before J decided to fly out to my neck of the woods- Denver, Colorado to see me for a few days. Once he arrived, a few days turned into months, and before I knew it, we were living together AND working together. A recipe for pure disaster and ultimate manipulation.

Section 2

Untangling a String of Red Flags

As soon as I mustered up the courage to finally pull the trigger and register for an LLC, J's manipulation took hold. I made everything official, using the first business name that came to my mind- Ring Relations. When I proudly shared this with J, I was met with a cold response.

"Wow, that's a terrible name. You should have called me before you did that," he said.

I was so perplexed. Isn't this what he wanted? How could taking this initiative on my own be 'wrong?'

Dissatisfied by my ability to make my own decisions, J kindly offered to help me secure my first real freelance client, putting himself in a position of power once again. It was a huge cannabis extraction company in California that was a recruiting client of J's. After the email introduction, I had a great solo call with the company CEO and quickly got to work.

Once the client signed the dotted line, I was off to the races, quickly securing several media hits and even landing their CEO a solo speaking presentation at the biggest cannabis industry conference that exists. Things were looking up when J offered to introduce me to another recruiting client of his.

I didn't realize how truly naive I was, thinking that he was helping me out of the kindness of his heart, until he came up with the idea of bundling his recruiting services with my PR consulting, giving himself a cut of the monthly PR retainer in the process. J always claimed to be similar to me in the sense that I genuinely strive to help people through my work, but once he noticed how much success I was having, he sang a different tune.

"You didn't really think I'd just hand you all of this business for nothing, did you?"

I can picture this exact moment so vividly in my head. I felt sick to my stomach, wondering how on earth I couldn't see something like this coming. It's fairly normal for agencies to offer something like a 'finding bonus' to people who secure business on their behalf, but this was different. He wanted to take a large percentage of my monthly income away from me, and convinced clients to pay him directly in the process. It was all a slippery slope from here as he gradually gained full control over the majority of my income.

Luckily, I wasn't left completely helpless. Throughout my time living with J and building up my book of business in cannabis, I had taken on a side project in a totally separate industry- domestic violence. Unlike my other projects, this one had nothing to do with J. But as I'd come to learn, it had everything to do with him.

It's hard for me to narrow it down to anything other than fate that led Caroline Markel-Hammond and me to rekindle our friendship. It had been years since we talked, but she was always someone in my life who I'd look at and think, "Can I just be you when I grow up?"

Naturally, when she opened up to me about her story and asked if it would make sense for us to work together, it had to have been the easiest "yes" in my life.

I'll never forget the moment when she explained the term 'gaslighting' to me, and described how her abuser used it to control and manipulate her. It sparked something in me. As someone who's required to write content, and carefully choose the right words to help companies get their message across, I have always been a glorified word nerd. Gaslighting was a new one to me, and I was fascinated by it. Words hold so much power. It's insane how much validity a simple term can provide.

I did everything I could to silence the alarm bells ringing in my head. I suddenly remembered all of those heated arguments that started with me asking a simple question. When are you going to send me my cut of the client retainer? Can you pay me your part of the rent? What exactly do you have against my friends? In response to these reasonable concerns, he would turn it around on me and make me feel guilty or out of line for questioning his actions.

As it turns out, I wasn't being crazy, I was Gaslit. I was Gaslit as all hell.

I truly wish I could say that upon realizing this, I broke off the toxic and abusive relationship, but of course, that's not the case. It's hardly ever the case. I was frozen in full-fledged denial mode, terrified of what the future of my career would look like if I forced J out of my life.

Then, a string of red flags began to appear. The red flags were waved by so many different people in my life. People who cared about me.

Red Flag #1

It started with Roger, the reporter who introduced me to J in the first place. When his messages started coming in, I was in rare form. I was enjoying myself at a bar with a few friends. No J. Ever since he moved in with me, unless it had something to do with work, I rarely saw anyone else. At that brief moment in time, I was free.

But I was quickly brought back down to earth when I started reading Roger's messages. He expressed some concerns about J a few months back. I was open with Roger when I was originally getting flustered with J, before anything romantic happened. The idea that I had never actually gotten paid for the PR work I had originally done for J in the very beginning really got under Roger's skin. I'd just brush it off and say it wasn't a big deal- he was helping me get business now and that's what mattered. At least, that's what I kept telling myself.

This time, when Roger raised the red flag to me, he came bearing proof of J's shady past.

He took screenshots of a conversation he had with one of J's former colleagues. This colleague opened up about how J never paid him for work he had done a few months back.

"See, I told you there was something not right with this guy," Roger said.

It's official. There's proof that what my abuser is doing to me is part of a pattern. I'm not the first to fall victim to his narcissism. Unfortunately, I wasn't in the right mindset to fully accept this information that was handed to me. Instead, I made the worst possible move I could make. I sent the screenshots to J and asked him to explain himself.

This sent J on a tirade. He knew he was caught. He knew what he had done was wrong, and that I was starting to connect the dots. So, what was J's next move? He set his sights on Roger, who as a journalist at a major, well-respected mainstream news publication, wielded too much power for J's liking.

Over the next 24 hours, it seemed like J spent every waking minute trying to reach the right person at Roger's massive workplace who could have Roger fired. I felt paralyzed by it all. I was put in a weird position and tensions were incredibly high between J and me as I begged him to just let it go. Later that week, Roger was fired. I was horrified at how skilled J was when it came to manipulating people to get whatever he wants. Perhaps more importantly, I was beyond disgusted by myself. How could I send those screenshots to J? Roger trusted me, and now he's jobless. Was I next?

Red Flag #2

Next enters the bold best friend. The type of friend who doesn't sugar coat things, but only because they truly love you. For me, that was Nicolette, aka 'Nico.' Whenever things got weird between us, especially when we lived together, Nico was always quick to nip it in the bud and address it right away. I always loved that about her, but when it came to unpacking her distaste for J, I could feel myself put up a wall between us that had never existed before. Nico could sense this new wall I had built, and in an attempt to tear it down, she asked me to meet her at our favorite diner for drinks. It had been a while since I saw her. J worked his magic to turn me against Nico, knowing full well that she wasn't blind to his bullshit.

"You need to stay focused; your friends are just distractions, and they don't understand what we're trying to build together," he would say.

When we sat down, she explained how she knew J was anything but 'the one' for me and expressed her concerns about my well-being. When things first became romantic with J, Nico was the first person I gushed to, claiming I was falling in love.

"But it wasn't that long ago when you said he was a nightmare!!" she said in utter disbelief, forcing me to remember what my life was like before the abuse began.

Honestly, I had yet to meet a guy who lived up to Nico's standards. Last time a love interest of mine failed Nico's test was just because he showed up to a BBQ wearing the most horrid jean jacket any of us had laid eyes on. This felt different than those other times, though. This was serious. She was trying to come to my rescue during a time when I didn't realize I needed saving.

Red Flag #3-#100

It didn't take long before more and more red flags continued to pile up faster than I could ignore them. Somewhere between the moment I spotted a bunch of incoming sexts pop up on his phone, and the moment a major client called to tell me that J had severely disrespected their CFO over a minor invoice issue, was my AHA moment. It came just in time for a big Europe trip I had in the books long before J blew up my life.

I should have been thanking my lucky stars that this trip came when it did, because it gave J a reason to finally go back to LA instead of hovering over my every move in Denver. Most victims who find themselves in these situations never experience this relief.

When I got back from Europe, I finally started to feel like myself again. Now that I had my privacy, I could have more candid conversations with clients about J. Unsurprisingly, none of them were fans, and the first client J introduced me to even came clean about how they were secretly working with other job recruiters but wanted to figure out how to keep working with me for PR.

But it really didn't matter what the clients thought at the end of the day, because even if I was doing good work, HE was the one receiving the payments. He took full advantage of that, eventually withholding my income for two months before I realized that he was probably never planning to pay me what I was owed.

At this point, I knew I needed to completely cut him out of my life, I just didn't know how, so I called a former boss/mentor of mine for advice. Shawna has been in the PR business for over 25 years, and she had been reaching out to me to see if I had any time to contract for the new agency she just launched. To this day, I'm beyond grateful for that conversation with Shawna. Not only did she provide me with work right away when J had left me cash poor, she connected me with a great employment lawyer who agreed to help me in my legal battle against J.

This legal battle was longer and way more expensive than I ever could have imagined, and eventually my legal bill was costing me more than the amount I was fighting to win. While I gradually lost all hope of ever getting the sweet revenge I so desperately wanted, I realized that in hindsight, I had already won. I was free from my abuser, completely, and I was doing all the things he kept telling me that I couldn't do - I was signing clients all on my own, without any of his help.

Section 3:

Giving a voice to the voiceless

It wasn't until recently that I called myself a 'survivor' for the very first time. It's strange that it took me so long to finally come out and say it, because, for the past four years, I've leveraged my PR superpowers to advocate for survivors. I've done my fair share of research and heard countless stories about what victims endure. Although some tend to follow similar patterns I personally encountered, no story is the same. Still, it felt slightly wrong to call myself a survivor of domestic violence. Why?

Because even though there were some moments when I thought J *might* physically abuse me, it never went that far.

My mindset was wrong in a lot of ways here, though. Not only should you avoid comparing your situation to that of others, but physical abuse also only represents one small percentage of domestic violence. This very notion was at the heart of several press releases and campaigns I've had the pleasure of working on for Safe in Harm's Way.

Today, I'm happy to coin myself a survivor. After all, I'm the one calling the shots, not my abuser. I came out on the other side of a horrible situation, and now I get to decide who I work with and how I do business. My first decision? Prioritize giving a voice to the voiceless by donating my services to Safe in Harm's Way. I've found great joy in using my strengths to help the nonprofit share the news about five national billboard campaigns that all aimed to bring victims closer to freedom. My hope is that if a victim doesn't see a billboard, digital ad, or social media post that speaks to their situation, maybe an article in Forbes, Newsweek, or Ms. Magazine will catch their eye, offering the resources they so desperately need. (Hot Tip: All of these publications have in fact featured Safe in Harm's Way.)

The caveat is that for every time a news headline comes to the rescue with useful information and quality journalism, it can just as easily do the opposite. Media love latching on to high-profile domestic violence court cases, such as the Depp v. Heard trial, but when it comes to offering up real solutions to readers, news headlines tend to fall short. This, I believe, is where I come in. As a publicist, I can play an important role in what's covered in the news. I say "can" because journalists are overworked, underpaid, and overwhelmed by thousands of emails from publicists per day. I love PR, but not because I think it's easy. I also love doing media relations for domestic violence organizations, but that's DEFINITELY not because it's easy.

It's because I know what it's like to shrink in fear of my abuser, like the woman pictured in the SIHW and Domestic Shelters 2022 campaign - *Feeling Small.* I watched it happen to my Mom when I was a kid as well.

PRESS RELEASE EXCERPT:

The PSA imagery thoughtfully uses the body language of a husband and wife sitting across the dinner table to spotlight the underlying scars of emotional abuse. The man in the image appears to be looming over the woman, physically encroaching in her space, while the woman is simultaneously shrinking in fear, discomfort, and shame. Along with the chilling image, is the take-home message that many abuse victims need to hear– "No one should make you feel small."

And I know what it's like to feel trapped with a monster who puts on a façade and doesn't fit the 'wife-beater' mold, which is what you see in the 2023 *Hidden Horrors* campaign. I do all of this because I want to keep history from repeating itself. Anyone who survives an abusive relationship deserves the opportunity to tell their story and be believed. I want to give them that chance, because they earned the right to be heard.

It's up to the rest of us to listen.

Kim Ring is a seasoned public relations professional with over nine years of experience, specializing in the cannabis industry after working with both large financial corporations and startups. Known as a 'PR Unicorn,' Kim has secured client coverage in top-tier publications like Wall Street Journal, Forbes, Newsweek, and USA Today.

A graduate of the University of Missouri with a B.A. in Communication and English, Kim began her career at Fleishman Hillard in St. Louis before moving to Denver to work as a Media Relations Specialist. She later became a Senior Publicist at Grasslands, leading PR efforts for cannabis businesses.

In 2019, Kim launched Ring Relations LLC, where she focuses on amplifying underrepresented voices. Her work includes leading national billboard campaigns for the domestic violence non-profit Safe In Harm's Way, where she also serves on the Board of Directors.

Kim's passion for food safety, stemming from her own experience with Celiac Disease, led her to her current role as Director of Communications at ASI. She also volunteers as Public Outreach Chair for the non-profit Show Me Food Safety based in her hometown of St. Louis.

TURNING GRIT INTO COURAGE

My heart was racing as I calmly turned and walked toward the door, got in my car and drove away. Minutes earlier I had arrived home to see his car in the driveway. I found him standing in the backyard chatting with the septic service tech. I asked him to leave. We were separated and he'd been stalking me for a few months.

At any time, day or night, I'd hear his 5-speed Mustang roar up and down the street. On several occasions I returned home to find evidence he had been there. A book on the perils of divorce on the front porch, a 6-page handwritten letter in the mailbox and once, he boldly left a large box inside the house subtly letting me know he could get in if he wanted to.

I was upset when I pulled into the driveway that day. What was he doing here? After I asked him to leave, I walked back toward the house. As I walked inside, his foot stopped the door from closing, and he followed me in the house. "You can't be here, please leave," I said firmly. His quick response startled me as he shouted, "THIS IS STILL MY HOUSE!" He took a step closer, and with a look in his eye I'd never seen before, he said, "In the eyes of God, we're still married. And, it wouldn't be wrong for us to have sex."

I felt a sinister chill come over the room. Having never experienced 'fight or flight' mode before, my body took over, and I calmly turned to walk toward the bathroom, *stay calm, don't run.* I kept walking until I reached the back door. *Run!* My heart was racing as I quickly got in my car, locked the doors and drove away. I was shaking all over. I was terrified he was going to rape me. My brother's words echoed in my head, "Do you think he is capable of hurting you?"

My first call was to the police, the second was to a locksmith. The police responded quickly and met me back at the house. I apologized several times for bothering them since he was gone and no longer threatening me. "You were right to call us," one officer said. My body heaved a big sigh of relief at his next words, "and I believe you."

He told me how dangerous stalking with domestic violence can be and promised to patrol the street when in the area.

After the officers left, I called and left a message with my lawyer. The police report, along with the large box full of his hand-delivered letters and other "gift" items he left while stalking me, convinced the judge to issue the restraining order I desperately needed.

When stalking and domestic violence intersect, the danger level for victims escalates quickly. According to SPARC (Stalking Awareness & Resource Center) 76 percent of femicide victims are stalked before being murdered. Stalking imbeds fear into your life like an ugly stench. Unknown sounds startle you. The triggers are hard to shed long after a victim has found safety. To this day, I must visually look to confirm every door is locked before going to bed each night.

After our 23-year marriage finally came to an end, I gradually began to regain my strength and my voice. Many victims don't realize they are in an abusive relationship. I knew my marriage was hard, but I didn't see the constant controlling of my everyday life - the gaslighting, humiliation, hurtful words, and use of scripture to control and shame me - as abusive. I never had bruises - on the outside. If only I had known earlier the signs of domestic violence in a relationship. The continual, daily drip, drip of emotional abuse and coercive control seeps into your head and changes how you think about everything. This explains how the strong women inside disappear, and the doubts, shame, and guilt take up residence instead.

I married right out of college to a man eight years older. He was charming and a minister, which appealed to me as a woman of faith. The marital relationship from the beginning was threaded throughout with spiritual abuse. What is that exactly, you might ask. With spiritual abuse, the dominant aggressor in an abusive relationship uses faith to control and maintain power over their partner. The abuser is always looking for ways, big and small, to control and impose power. In a relationship marred by spiritual abuse, defiance is met with shame, guilt and God-fearing opposition. With every haircut, I was told women were to have long hair simply because that's what he preferred. But he used scripture to justify his control. My refusal to apologize for a haircut was met with silence - two to three days of existing without being noticed or spoken to AT ALL. When my punishment was complete, he would come to me with his Bible in hand and read from Colossians, women are to have long, flowing hair.

A similar response came when I disagreed, challenged his request, or defied his demand. It could be hours to days later, and with his Bible in hand he would choose Ephesians 5, "wives be subject to your husbands." But he conveniently left off the following part saying husbands must love their wives as Christ loved the church.

It wasn't until years later that I accepted the fact there was physical, sexual and reproductive abuse in the marriage. The physical abuse came when he approached me with ill intent to show he had all the power. As I washed dishes or prepared dinner, he walked up to me and groped one breast so hard his other hand had to go behind my back to prevent me from falling backwards. My objection was quick and direct. He responded by quoting scripture "...the two shall become one flesh" which meant my body was his as we were one, and that he had unfettered access. To be sure, this was never an act of love or even, I dare say, foreplay. It was a direct message to me that he 'owned' my body, and I had no say in the matter. My objections and rebuke were met with being told I was a bad wife and an ice queen.

He became the lead pastor of a church of over 10,000 people. He was powerful. And beloved. As I observed other marriages and compared them to mine, I knew my marriage was hard, exhausting, but I never thought of it as abusive. Being married in the early '80s, domestic violence was never the topic du jour. Emergency shelters were just beginning to pop up through the efforts of women's groups, church groups and community responses. No one talked about their difficult marriage. Domestic violence was violent, right?

I'm sometimes asked to describe the pinnacle moment that convinced me to leave the marriage. It's hard to say there is just one, it becomes a progression of events that lead you to a dark place. Eventually, I found myself emotionally pulling away from the marriage, venturing perilously close to the edge of darkness and despair. Then, on Valentine's Day, I received a gift. This gift, just a couple years later, won the 'worst Valentine's Day gift ever' award on a radio show. My husband gave me the book by one of his favorite authors, Dr. Laura Schlesinger. The unbelievable title - "The Proper Care and Feeding of Husbands." And to make it even more romantic, he had highlighted parts he especially thought I should read. I know. It's hard to believe.

His gift essentially released the trap door to a dark hole of depression.

I finally mustered up the courage to leave. From the moment I said, "I want a divorce" to the sound of the judge's gavel declaring it final, existed a time warp of delays, denials, stalking and shocking vitriol. My well-worn grit propelled me to my freedom, finally being used for a positive end. A few years after the divorce, I was invited to serve on the board of the second largest domestic violence agency in Texas. As board chair, I read the annual Fatality Review for our county revealing most DV homicide victims had not reached out for help, not even by calling the hotline. This disturbed me to my core. I couldn't sleep for several nights. How could this be? The seeds for raising awareness were planted.

I knew deep within my bones I had to do something to raise awareness. But how? How can one survivor make a difference?

I had a crazy idea to make a movie. I never dreamed of being a filmmaker, but as I approached my 60th birthday, I jumped into the movie making world to raise awareness with no idea of the adventure that lay ahead.

I poured my experience of an abusive marriage into becoming a first-time filmmaker to raise awareness with the movie. As executive producer of *No Ordinary Love*, I showed up on set for the first day of filming eager to see how this process plays out. Months of preparation led to this day. The script was written, casting complete, filming locations contracted, crew in place - and I hear "Sounds up.... camera ready...aaannd ACTION!"

I asked two things from the film's auteur writer/director. I wanted the script to portray an authentic and realistic view of domestic violence, and also to highlight spiritual abuse. Even in the domestic violence advocacy world, spiritual abuse is often given a cursory nod but not fully embraced for its destructive nature to victims. If my goal was to raise awareness of intimate partner violence, I wanted the audience to especially see and understand how one's faith can be the vehicle of power and control.

Creating an indie film is harder and more challenging than I could have ever imagined. I honestly had no idea what the two plus years would entail from pre-filming stage to postproduction, film festivals and finally signing with a distributor. Prior to the film streaming, *USA Today* named it one of the "Biggest Summer Movies" of 2021. I wanted to use the film to raise even more awareness. I thought back to the time I was a young woman who naively fell into an abusive relationship. What if I had seen this film while I was in college? What if I had heard someone speak about healthy relationships and red flags for abuse? Could I have avoided being married to an abusive man? I've made *No Ordinary Love* available to college campuses and domestic violence organizations to raise awareness. Military bases, police academies, seminaries and any community group could use this film to open eyes and raise awareness.

So now what? I ask myself this question every day. I have a burning desire to go upstream. We spend so much money, effort, entire careers managing and addressing male violence against women. But we need to go upstream on this issue. The whole male issue that contributes to domestic violence will take decades to change. I want to help parents better prepare their daughters for teenage and young adult dating.

We can teach young women to know the signs of a healthy partner, to *be* a healthy partner, and to hone their radars to see the red flags that are signs of an abusive relationship early enough to avoid being love bombed into one.

Our whole existence, culture, traditions, history and societies have been built on patriarchy. Male violence against women is an immortal issue. As a rule, women, throughout all of time, have had to be vigilant, always on guard against violent, abusive and powerful men. Always. Most men do not understand this level of alertness. But we know, as women, we are not safe to walk most streets at night without fear of being sexually assaulted. Some of us are not safe when we go home to an abusive partner or go to work to possibly be sexually harassed. When we go shopping or to the grocery store, we avoid parking next to a white, windowless work-van for fear of being abducted into human trafficking. We are always vigilant, and we teach this to our daughters.

We can persist in sheltering victims and holding offenders accountable, creating new laws to protect women and funding programs to keep them safe. But to create the necessary social changes, we must rip up the roots of domestic violence by demanding and creating gender equality. Only when both women and men are at all tables where decisions are made - will gender equality become the eternal and lived truth for everyone. When men and women are truly equal in power, authority and governance, then we can hope for domestic violence to be left behind us and attain a peaceful and safe existence for all.

Tracy Rector, speaker, film producer, author, and survivor, uses her voice to raise awareness of gender-based violence. As an international speaker, she's shared her energy inspiring audiences in the US including Guam, Asia Pacific, and UK. She's especially passionate about giving young adults the tools to have a healthy relationship and to recognize signs of abuse.

At both in-person and virtual events, she threads her personal story of domestic abuse in her message and invites all to join her in a front-row seat to the issue. Her words resonate with audiences as a significant number of women and men are affected by domestic violence in their lifetime.

USA Today recognized her film, No Ordinary Love, as one of the "biggest summer movies" of 2021. The film, using survivor stories, including her own, shines an authentic spotlight on domestic violence.

She created an educational program for college campuses, domestic violence agencies and other groups using the film to raise awareness. She served as board chair of the second largest domestic violence agency in Texas, and she is currently part of a research project involving national industry leaders to develop a game-changing, potentially life-saving tool to identify the dominant aggressor in domestic violence incidents.

CONTACT INFO
tracy.rector@gmail.com
project-raiseawareness.com
Facebook: TracyRector1
Twitter: @TracyRector1
Instagram: tracytrector
LinkedIn: Tracy Rector (Speaker, Producer, Author, Survivor)

LOOPED SOLUTIONS™ - INNOVATING CONNECTION: FOR LIFE, FOR COMMUNITY, FOR BUSINESS

The Journey Begins

My journey to entrepreneurship and developing technology solutions for social care began in 2016 as a result of experiencing communication challenges during an important family event. My little sister had gone into labor, and I was accidentally left off of the group text informing close family and friends that the baby was coming. In the meantime, I had left town resulting in me ultimately not being able to be present for the birth of my niece. The chaos began the moment I was added to the group. I had absolutely no idea who else was in this group because I didn't have phone numbers saved for the others in the group to identify them. I had to scroll to find important information that was lost between chatter. The entire experience felt impersonal, chaotic, and stressful. So, while I was experiencing this chaos, I started looking in the app store for a mobile waiting room app. I was surprised to find that there weren't any existing apps designed to be set up long before going into labor that could have made it easy for users to be updated all at the same time privately. Despite having no background in technology, I knew then that I needed to create a solution to solve this problem.

As a real estate lender for a local bank for 15 years, I had a promising career ahead of me, but I was being pulled in another direction with this idea. While I was sorting out what to do next, a colleague mentioned that he had a friend who has a web design business, and who coincidentally wanted to get into mobile development. He told me I should call her. So, I did. That call marked the very beginning of the journey.

In 2019, After securing pre-seed funding from a PA based economic development group, I was able to invest in the necessary resources to develop the app, including identifying a development company and adding a development leader to the existing team of 1. Me. Soon afterwards, we raised additional funding that allowed me to begin to design the team I needed to go to market.

In mid-2020, OhanaLink Technologies first entered the market launching our first mobile app, OhanaLink™, a mobile app that connects family and friends during healthcare events. Shortly after launching the OhanaLink App, the need for technology for social care agencies was brought to our company's attention. We were in the early days of the Covid-19 pandemic when we were approached by the executive director of a local domestic violence agency asking if our existing platform could be adapted to help advocates and victims of domestic abuse connect safely. Their phones had stopped ringing. Victims were in the homes with their abusers sometimes 24/7 due to covid lockdowns. The old methods of service delivery were no longer ideal, and this category of non-profit social service agencies had been historically underserved with respect to technology. When presented with this unique opportunity, we quickly committed to collaborating on the design of a safe, secure system for agencies and victims/survivors. We engaged with agencies in Western Pennsylvania to understand the challenges facing advocates and victims of domestic violence and how the lack of safety and privacy in the existing technology can result in life and death situations for many victims of abuse.

As a result of this collaboration, we launched OhanaLink Purple, recently rebranded as Looped Fusion Purple™, in May of 2022 and on-boarded our first agencies shortly after. Looped Fusion Purple enables safe communication and collaboration between service providers and their clients on any smart/mobile device (phone or tablet). We built specially designed features that connect service providers with their clients within a single communication and engagement system enabling victims to safely access the resources they need—even if they are being tracked or monitored on their devices. The product is being adopted by agencies across the U.S. enabling advocates to provide access to OhanaLink Purple to the clients they serve.

Our Company's Evolution

This year marked OhanaLink Technologies' 5-year entrance into the market and we knew it was time for a change. Over the course of our journey, we spoke to hundreds of agencies and organizations and witnessed firsthand the growing need for solutions that **innovate the connections** that encompass how we live, how we work, and how we engage with our most valued networks and communities. We are extremely proud of what we have accomplished and how we have proactively responded to emerging market demands in healthcare, social care, victim services, education, and life events.

We believe this market dynamic afforded us new opportunities to diversify our portfolio of services and expand our customer base to encompass both for profits and non-profit organizations. With all of that in mind, OhanaLink Technologies embarked on a comprehensive analysis of our market presence including our brand and our go-to-market and business strategies and determined it was time for a bold move. We engaged an outside consulting firm to assist with research and strategic direction for the next generation of OhanaLink Technologies.

As a result, we were thrilled to reintroduce ourselves as Looped Solutions™ - designing innovative technology that keeps us "looped in" to how we live, how we work, and how we engage with our most valued networks and communities.

Why Looped Solutions?

Our daily activities vary but include the ongoing development and support of our products, continued market awareness through education and outreach to state coalitions, victim services providers, and industry thought leaders, as well as providing customer support, education and training to ensure user success.

"Great things in business are never done by one person. They're done by a team of people". (Steve Jobs)

Establishing my team has been the most important step in building this business. I knew very early on in this process that I needed to surround myself with people that brought the skills and knowledge to the table that I needed to take this vision and company forward.

I am so grateful to have the opportunity to do what I do every day alongside my brilliant team. I would not be here at this point in time without them and I certainly wouldn't be here without the support of our investors who believed in all of us. Each one of them has taken a risk to trust me and my vision and that is not lost on me. They are the REAL world changers.

Our Mission

Our mission is to design solutions that innovate the connections encompassing how we live, how we work, and how we engage with our most valued networks and communities.

As someone whose family has been affected by domestic abuse, developing Looped Fusion Purple has been a deeply personal and meaningful endeavor. I am incredibly grateful for the opportunity to address a global issue that has directly impacted many of my loved ones. Additionally, several members of our team have shared their own experiences with domestic violence and view this work as a powerful way to give back and help others in need.

Our Roadmap

At Looped Solutions, we are reimagining traditional communication and engagement systems for victim service providers. Our commitment is to develop products that prioritize safety and privacy for both advocates and victims.

We've made significant progress on our product roadmap, including the recent launch of feature enhancements and a web-based version of Looped Fusion Purple. This new version is designed to drive adoption, particularly for advocates who may not have access to or prefer not to use their personal mobile devices.

As we continue to grow, we're also revisiting our roots by revitalizing our premier mobile solution, the OhanaLink app. There's still a strong demand and market opportunity for what we initially built, but as a startup, we prioritized addressing the immediate need for safe technology solutions for victims and the service providers who support them.

Committed to Transforming Service Delivery

We continue to invest in both the technology behind Looped Fusion as well as developing new tools and resources to better support our agency partners. We are committed to enhancing the lives of our users through the use of our solutions and are dedicated to partnering with organizations, agencies and associations to enable new delivery systems to support victims/survivors of abuse of all types as well as their support systems.

Creating A New Paradigm

As a relatively new tech company with new products, much of our resources are spent on education and raising awareness about our mission, our vision and the benefits of our solutions to a wide range of stakeholders.

We understand the importance of having the right contacts and making connections with those who can influence change. Our strategy is to collaborate with industry leaders and others who are making important contributions to the international movement against domestic violence. Partnerships such as those we now have with Vela and PurpleOne (purpleone.org) to create integrations that streamline and centralize tools, resources, and technology under one single delivery system are where others can add value.

In summary, we value the relationships we have built to date, but also realize it takes a village to make real change. It takes one phone call, one email to the right person that can make all the difference. We invite others to join us as we build these connections. One tool, one resource, one idea at a time!

About Looped Solutions™

Looped Solutions is a women-led tech company that is designing cross-platform applications - innovating connections surrounding every aspect of our lives—personally, professionally, and in our communities. At the very core of our innovation is Looped Launchpad, our proprietary platform that powers our digital engagement solutions. Fusion, the Company's central offering, empowers effective communication and collaboration by merging a collection of features specifically designed to ignite connection and engagement. For tailored solutions, our Fusion bundles, such as Fusion Purple for social care and victim services and Fusion White Label for developing branded applications, provide customizable options that close the loop on achieving goals. At Looped Solutions, we are dedicated to delivering flexible solutions to meet individual needs, ensuring seamless connections to who and what matter most.

Discover how our solutions can transform how we live, work, and engage at http://www.loopedsolutions.com

Kara Wasser, Founder and CEO
Looped Solutions
Email: kw@loopedsolutions.com
Office: 844-394-4398
Website: www.loopedsolutions.com

www.ingramcontent.com/pod-product-compliance
Lightning Source LLC
LaVergne TN
LVHW010105170826
845678LV00012B/2245

* 9 7 9 8 2 1 8 5 5 2 0 8 4 *